HOUGHTON MIFFLIN

Enjoy

INVITATIONS TO LITERACY

Houghton Mifflin Company • Boston

Atlanta • Dallas • Geneva, Illinois • Palo Alto • Princeton

www.bookadventure.org

read.

Use the on-line "Book Finder" to find a book you want to read.

click.

After reading, return on-line to take a fun interactive quiz.

win.

For every correct answer, you can earn points. Redeem the points for prizes.

When you read, use these Reading Strategies to become a better reader.

- Predict/Infer
- Think About Words
- Self-Question
- Monitor
- Evaluate
- Summarize

HOUGHTON MIFFLIN

Enjoy

Senior Authors

J. David Cooper
John J. Pikulski

Authors

Kathryn H. Au
Margarita Calderón
Jacqueline C. Comas
Marjorie Y. Lipson
J. Sabrina Mims
Susan E. Page
Sheila W. Valencia
MaryEllen Vogt

Consultants

Dolores Malcolm
Tina Saldivar
Shane Templeton

Houghton Mifflin Company • Boston

Atlanta • Dallas • Geneva, Illinois • Palo Alto • Princeton

Cover and title page photography by Tim Turner.

Cover illustration from *A Fruit & Vegetable Man* by Roni Schotter, illustrated by Jeanette Winter. Illustration copyright © 1993 by Jeanette Winter. Reprinted by permission of Little, Brown & Company.

Acknowledgments appear on page 318.

Printed in the U.S.A.

ISBN: 0-618-05786-2

23456789-VH-05 04 03 02 01 00

Enjoy AT A GLANCE

Oink,
Oink,
Oink

CONTENTS

Community Ties

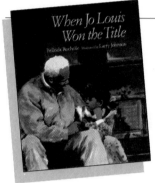

PAPERBACK **PLUS**

My Buddy
fiction by
Audrey Osofsky

In the same book . . .
poetry and an article about a dog trainer

Cam Jansen and the Mystery of the Babe Ruth Baseball
a mystery by David A. Adler

In the same book . . .
card-collecting tips and statistics

CONTENTS

DISASTER!

HARRY ALLARD
MISS NELSON IS MISSING!
TEXAS
JAMES MARSHALL

The kids in Room 207 were misbehaving again. Spitballs stuck to the ceiling. Paper planes whizzed through the air. They were the worst-behaved class in the whole school.

"Now settle down," said Miss Nelson in a sweet voice.

But the class would *not* settle down. They whispered and giggled. They squirmed and made faces. They were even rude during story hour. And they always refused to do their lessons.

"Something will have to be done," said Miss Nelson.

The next morning Miss Nelson did not come to school. "Wow!" yelled the kids. "Now we can *really* act up!" They began to make more spitballs and paper planes. "Today let's be just terrible!" they said.

"Not so fast!" hissed an unpleasant voice.

A woman in an ugly black dress stood before them. "I am your new teacher, Miss Viola Swamp." And she rapped the desk with her ruler.

"Where is Miss Nelson?" asked the kids.

"Never mind that!" snapped Miss Swamp. "Open those arithmetic books!" Miss Nelson's kids did as they were told.

WORK
TO BE DONE
1. MATH
2. POEMS
3. ENGLISH
4. HISTORY
5. GEOGRAPHY

They could see that Miss Swamp was a real witch. She meant business.

Right away she put them to work. And she loaded them down with homework.

“We’ll have no story hour today,” said Miss Swamp.

“Keep your mouths shut,” said Miss Swamp.

“Sit perfectly still,” said Miss Swamp.

“And if you misbehave, you’ll be sorry,” said Miss Swamp.

The kids in Room 207 had *never* worked so hard.

Days went by and there was no sign of Miss Nelson. The kids *missed* Miss Nelson!

“Maybe we should try to find her,” they said. Some of them went to the police.

Detective McSmogg was assigned to the case. He listened to their story. He scratched his chin. “Hmmmm,” he said. “Hmmm. I think Miss Nelson is missing.”

Detective McSmogg would not be much help.

Other kids went to Miss Nelson's house. The shades were tightly drawn, and no one answered the door. In fact, the only person they *did* see was the wicked Miss Viola Swamp, coming up the street.

"If she sees us, she'll give us more homework." They got away just in time.

Maybe something *terrible* happened to Miss Nelson! "Maybe she was gobbled up by a shark!" said one of the kids. But that didn't seem likely.

"Maybe Miss Nelson went to Mars!" said another kid. But that didn't seem likely either.

"I know!" exclaimed one know-it-all. "Maybe Miss Nelson's car was carried off by a swarm of angry butterflies!" But that was the least likely of all.

The kids in Room 207 became very discouraged. It seemed that Miss Nelson was never coming back. And they would be stuck with Miss Viola Swamp forever.

They heard footsteps in the hall. "Here comes the witch," they whispered.

"Hello, children," someone said in a sweet voice.

It was Miss Nelson! "Did you miss me?" she asked.

"We certainly did!" cried all the kids. "Where were you?"

"That's my little secret," said Miss Nelson. "How about a story hour?"

"Oh, yes!" cried the kids.

Miss Nelson noticed that during story hour no one was rude or silly. "What brought about this lovely change?" she asked.

"That's *our* little secret," said the kids.

Back home Miss Nelson took off her coat and hung it in the closet (right next to an ugly black dress).

When it was time for bed she sang a little song. “I’ll never tell,” she said to herself with a smile.

P. S. Detective McSmogg is working on a new case. He is *now* looking for Miss Viola Swamp.

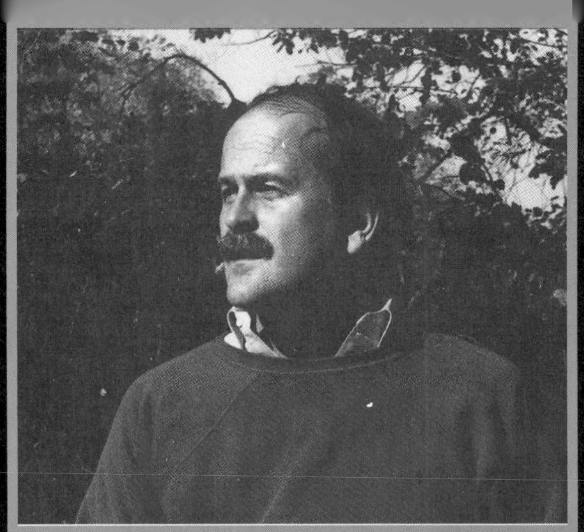

Meet the Author
Harry Allard

Harry Allard is always writing something. He keeps a diary. He writes a lot of letters. And, of course, he writes books. When Allard gets an idea for a story, he just begins writing. Even if it's three in the morning.

Meet the Illustrator
James Marshall

How would you like to have Miss Viola Swamp for a teacher? James Marshall once said that he had a second grade teacher like her. In fact, when he drew Miss Swamp, he kept his teacher in mind.

Harry Allard and James Marshall were a team for almost twenty years. Two other popular books by them are The Stupids Step Out *and* Miss Nelson Is Back.

Investigating the Story

Put On a Puppet Show

Settle Down, Class!

What might Miss Nelson and Miss Swamp say to *your* class? Make puppets of them. Then, with a partner, make up things for them to say.

Make a Poster

Wanted: Miss Viola Swamp

Help Detective McSmogg find Miss Viola Swamp. Create a "Wanted" poster. Be sure to include a picture of her and a description of the way she acts.

Oink, Oink, Oink

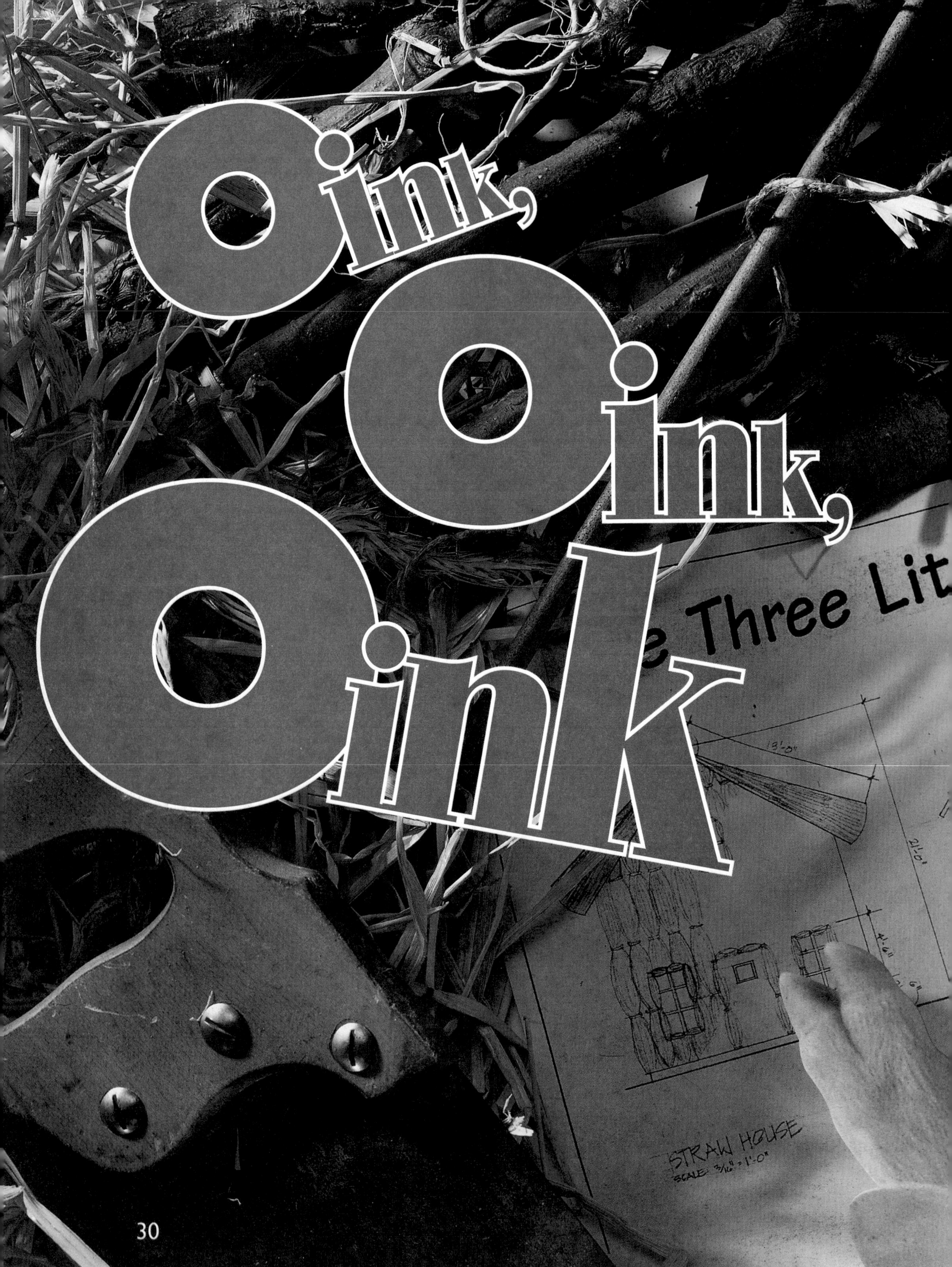

e Pigs' Houses
13'-0"
13'-0"
21'-0"
21'-0"
4'-6"

Oink, Oink, Oink Contents

Oink, Oink, Oink Read On Your Own

PAPERBACK **PLUS**

Sidney Rella and the Glass Sneaker

by Bernice Myers

When Sidney wants to be a football star, his fairy godfather helps out.

In the same book . . .

The original "Cinderella," plus a photo guessing game to keep you on your toes.

Sleeping Ugly

by Jane Yolen

Plain Jane's no beauty. Will the prince awaken her?

In the same book . . .

The unfractured version, plus some tired old jokes.

Books to Squeal About

All Pigs Are Beautiful
by Dick King-Smith
This author loves pigs. For the first time, he explains why.

The Great Pig Escape
by Eileen Christelow
When Bert's pigs hear they're bound to be bacon, they make a break for it.

The True Story of the 3 Little Pigs
by Jon Scieszka
The wolf finally gets to tell *his* side of the story.

The Three Little Pigs and the Fox
by William H. Hooks
It's suppertime, and this fox is in the mood for pork chops.

WATCH ME READ
Goldie Bear and the Three Locks

WATCH ME READ
Ham and Eggs for Jack

WATCH ME READ
Red Riding Hood and Gray Wolf

About the Author

Eugene Trivizas

has written many books — but in Greek. *The Three Little Wolves and the Big Bad Pig* is the first book he wrote in English. Eugene lives part of the year in Greece and part of the year in England. He has written about many subjects, including football and crime.

About the Illustrator

Helen Oxenbury

has always loved to draw and paint. She once had a job drawing pictures for birthday cards and other greeting cards you buy in stores. Now she lives with her family in London, England, and illustrates books for children.

EUGENE TRIVIZAS
HELEN OXENBURY
The
Three Little Wolves
and the
Big Bad Pig

Once upon a time, there were three cuddly little wolves with soft fur and fluffy tails who lived with their mother. The first was black, the second was gray, and the third was white.

One day the mother called the three little wolves around her and said, “My children, it is time for you to go out into the world. Go and build a house for yourselves. But beware of the big bad pig.”

“Don’t worry, Mother, we will watch out for him,” said the three little wolves, and they set off.

Soon they met a kangaroo who was pushing a wheelbarrow full of red and yellow bricks.

"Please, will you give us some of your bricks?" asked the three little wolves.

"Certainly," said the kangaroo, and she gave them lots of red and yellow bricks.

So the three little wolves built themselves a house of bricks.

The very next day the big bad pig came prowling down the road and saw the house of bricks that the little wolves had built.

The three little wolves were playing croquet in the garden. When they saw the big bad pig coming, they ran inside the house and locked the door.

The pig knocked on the door and grunted, "Little wolves, little wolves, let me come in!"

"No, no, no," said the three little wolves. "By the hair on our chinny-chin-chins, we will not let you in, not for all the tea leaves in our china teapot!"

"Then I'll huff and I'll puff and I'll blow your house down!" said the pig.

So he huffed and he puffed and he puffed and he huffed, but the house didn't fall down.

But the pig wasn't called big and bad for nothing. He went and fetched his sledgehammer, and he knocked the house down.

The three little wolves only just managed to escape before the bricks crumbled, and they were very frightened indeed.

"We shall have to build a stronger house," they said.

Just then they saw a beaver who was mixing concrete in a concrete mixer.

"Please, will you give us some of your concrete?" asked the three little wolves.

"Certainly," said the beaver, and he gave them buckets and buckets full of messy, slurry concrete.

So the three little wolves built themselves a house of concrete.

No sooner had they finished than the big bad pig came prowling down the road and saw the house of concrete that the little wolves had built.

They were playing battledore and shuttlecock in the garden, and when they saw the big bad pig coming, they ran inside their house and shut the door.

The pig rang the bell and said, "Little frightened wolves, let me come in!"

"No, no, no," said the three little wolves. "By the hair on our chinny-chin-chins, we will not let you in, not for all the tea leaves in our china teapot."

"Then I'll huff and I'll puff and I'll blow your house down!" said the pig.

So he huffed and he puffed and he puffed and he huffed, but the house didn't fall down.

But the pig wasn't called big and bad for nothing. He went and fetched his pneumatic drill and smashed the house down.

The three little wolves managed to escape, but their chinny-chin-chins were trembling and trembling and trembling.

"We shall build an even stronger house," they said, because they were very determined. Just then they saw a truck coming along the road carrying barbed wire, iron bars, armor plates, and heavy metal padlocks.

"Please, will you give us some of your barbed wire, a few iron bars and armor plates, and some heavy metal padlocks?" they said to the rhinoceros who was driving the truck.

"Sure," said the rhinoceros, and he gave them plenty of barbed wire, iron bars, armor plates, and heavy metal padlocks. He also gave them some Plexiglas and some reinforced steel chains, because he was a generous and kind-hearted rhinoceros.

So the three little wolves built themselves an extremely strong house. It was the strongest, securest house one could possibly imagine. They felt absolutely safe.

The next day the big bad pig came prowling along the road as usual. The three little wolves were playing hopscotch in the garden. When they saw the big bad pig coming, they ran inside their house, bolted the door, and locked all the thirty-seven padlocks.

The pig dialed the video entrance phone and said, "Little frightened wolves with the trembling chins, let me come in!"

"No, no, no!" said the little wolves. "By the hair on our chinny-chin-chins, we will not let you in, not for all the tea leaves in our china teapot."

"Then I'll huff and I'll puff and I'll blow your house down!" said the pig.

So he huffed and he puffed and he puffed and he huffed, but the house didn't fall down.

But the pig wasn't called big and bad for nothing. He rented a crane, drove it to the house, swung the wrecking ball as high as it could go, and . . .

he demolished the house. The three little wolves just managed to escape with their fluffy tails flattened.

"Something must be wrong with our building materials," they said. "We have to try something different. But *what?*"

At that moment they saw a flamingo coming along pushing a wheelbarrow full of flowers.

"Please, will you give us some flowers?" asked the little wolves.

"With pleasure," said the flamingo, and he gave them lots of flowers. So the three little wolves built themselves a house of flowers.

One wall was of marigolds, one of daffodils, one of pink roses, and one of cherry blossoms. The ceiling was made of sunflowers, and the floor was a carpet of daisies. They had water lilies in their bathtub, and buttercups in their refrigerator. It was a rather fragile house and it swayed in the wind, but it was very beautiful.

Next day the big bad pig came prowling down the road and saw the house of flowers that the three little wolves had built.

He rang the bluebell at the door and said, "Little frightened wolves with the trembling chins and the flattened tails, let me come in!"

"No, no, no," said the three little wolves. "By the hair on our chinny-chin-chins, we will not let you in, not for all the tea leaves in our china teapot!"

"Then I'll huff and I'll puff and I'll blow your house down!" said the pig.

But as he took a deep breath, ready to huff and puff, he smelled the soft scent of the flowers. It was fantastic. And because the scent was so lovely, the pig took another breath and then another. Instead of huffing and puffing, he began to sniff.

He sniffed deeper and deeper until he was quite filled with the fragrant scent. His heart grew tender, and he realized how horrible he had been. Right then he decided to become a big *good* pig.

He started to sing and to dance the tarantella.

At first the three little wolves were a bit worried. It might be a trick. But soon they realized that the pig had truly changed, so they came running out of the house.

They started playing games with him.

First they played pig-pog and then piggy-in-the-middle, and when they were all tired, they invited him into the house.

They offered him tea and strawberries and wolfberries, and asked him to stay with them as long as he wanted.

The pig accepted, and they all lived happily together ever after.

Building on the Story

Design a House

Home, Sweet Home

What else other than flowers could turn a big bad pig into a big *good* pig? With a partner, design a new house made out of something that looks, smells, or tastes really good.

Tell a Story

Twice Upon a Time

Think of another story you can turn inside out. Maybe the Three Bears pay a visit to Goldilocks' house or Little Red Riding Hood dresses like the wolf's granny.

What's UP, Pup?

by Lyle Prescott
photos by Art Wolfe

Eight-week-old gray wolf pups are usually busy little creatures. Luckily, this one is sitting still long enough for us to get a good look. Gretta is her name, and she's taking a break after a morning romp. She won't rest for long, though. What's next? Turn the page to see what kind of mischief she might stir up.

Ranger Rick

Chomp! "OK, grass — you haven't got a chance against a tough wolf like me," Gretta might be thinking (**right**). Like other young wolf pups, she likes to play with and explore almost everything around her. (She may even eat the grass after she finishes "attacking" it.)

Gretta is also practicing using her teeth. See those pointy ones at the sides of her mouth? They're called *canines* (KAY-nines), and they'll help her hunt when she gets older.

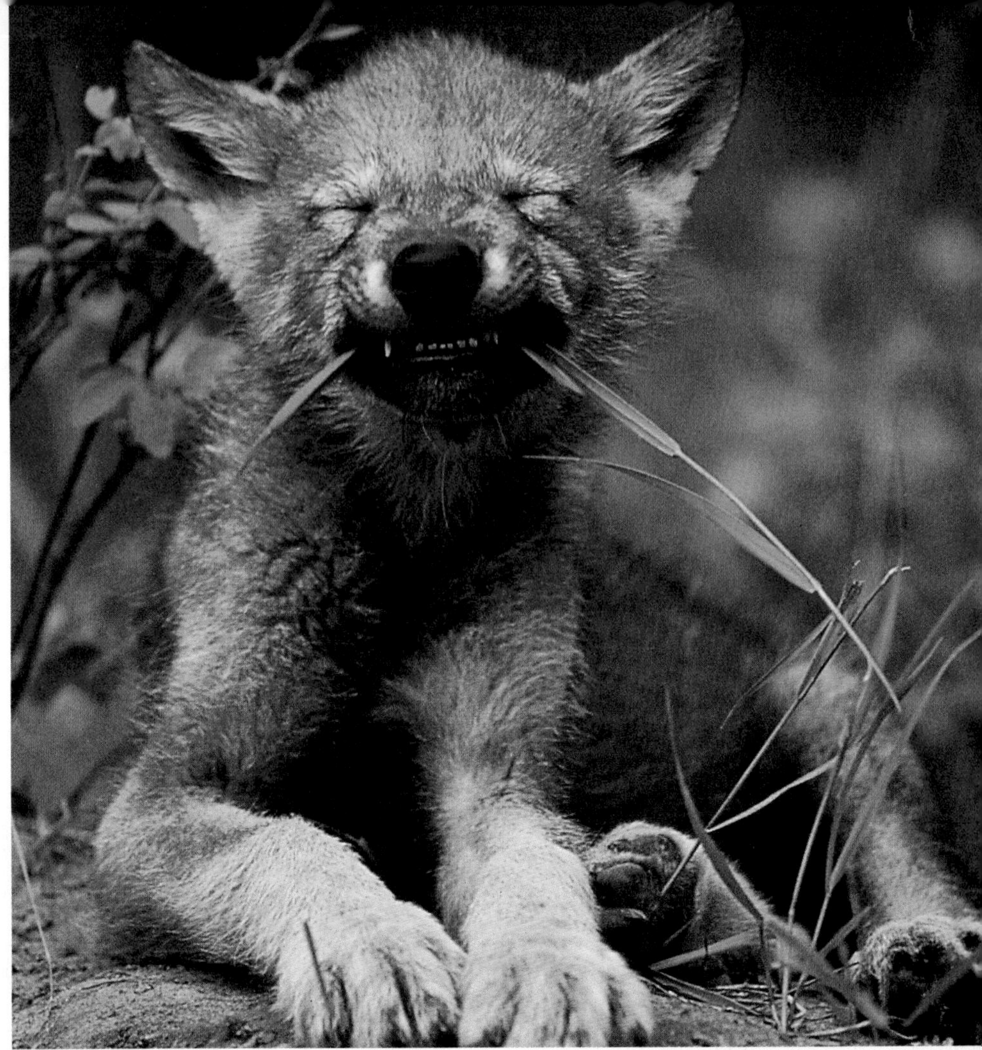

Every day, wolf pups tumble and wrestle together (**left**). Playing like this helps the pups figure out which ones will later be bosses and which ones will get bossed around. Plus, the fast-growing pups need to exercise their muscles. By the time autumn comes, they'll have to be strong enough to join the adults at hunting time.

The other frisky wolf pups have dashed off without Gretta. They couldn't have gone far — but where are they? She throws back her head and lets out a long, sad howl (**right**). "Hey, guys, you left me here all alone — *please* come back," the little pup seems to be calling.

A wolf may howl alone, or a pack may howl together in a chorus. Either way, the sounds can carry for a long distance. Sometimes wolves may howl messages to each other from a mile or two apart.

The wolf pups like to hang out all over Mom (**above**). That's Gretta in front, giving Mom a lick. Luckily for the little pups, the adult wolves are never too old to play.

It oinks! It wallows! It hangs out with the litter! Here's all the dirt on . . .

This Little Piggy!

by Linda Granfield

Can pigs swim?

What good are pigs' snouts?

Are pigs smart?

Are all pigs born with curly tails?

Do pigs prefer to be dirty?

Do pigs really make pigs of themselves?

Go hog wild. Take a look at these questions and see how many you can answer. If you think pigs are hard to peg down, you're right!

Pigs swim on hot, sunny days.

You might be surprised to know that pigs are great dog paddlers! Sometimes, they'll escape the burning sun by taking a swim at a water hole. The large amount of fat in their bodies helps keep even heavy pigs floating in the water. Pigs are such good swimmers they can cross rivers many kilometers (miles) wide.

A pig's snout is a pig's best friend.

Sure, a pig's snout is used for breathing — but it's also great for sweating, digging, and reaching out to other pigs! Like a dog, a pig sweats through its nose instead of its skin. A pig counts on its snout's flat front and bony upper rim as it digs in the dirt and unearths tasty roots. But all that digging doesn't harden a pig's nose. It remains moist and tender — perfect for greeting another pig snout-to-snout when they meet!

When Pigs Fly

Pigs have trotted their way into many of our expressions. See if you can match each of these with its meaning. Then check your answers on page 66.

1. pigpen	a. stubborn
2. pig-headed	b. braid
3. go whole hog	c. living well
4. pigtail	d. never
5. high off the hog	e. messy place
6. when pigs fly	f. take to the limit

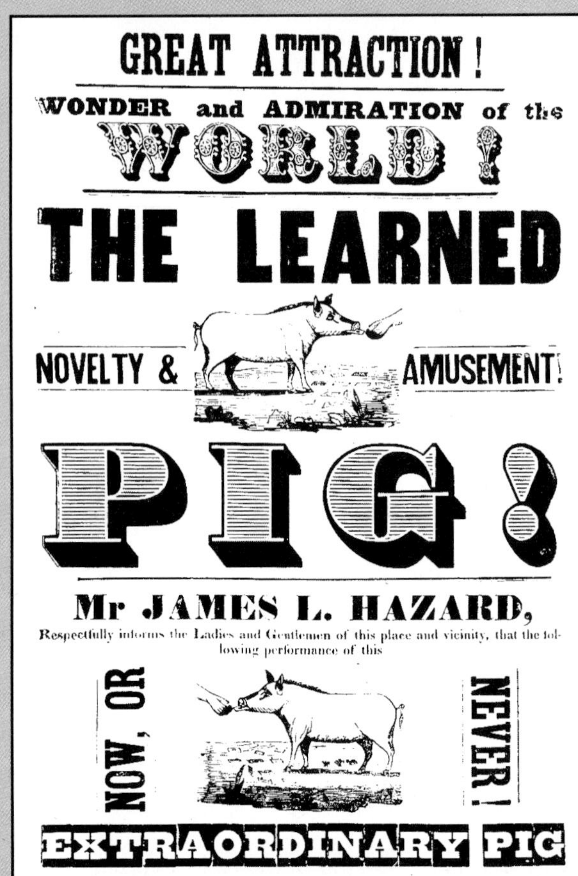

Straight or curly pig tails tell tales.

Many, but not all, breeds of pigs are born with curly tails. But when a kinky-tailed pig is scared or not feeling well, its tail may straighten out. Do all curly pig tails curl in the same direction? One old American saying claims that pigs' tails in the south twist clockwise, while pigs' tails in the north twist the opposite way.

Pigs are smarter than you think!

Pigs were one of the first animals to be trained by people. In 1785, a famous hog, called the Learned Pig, was taught to spell words, tell time, and solve math problems with the help of rewards. Today, some scientists believe that pigs are very intelligent and easier to train than dogs. They report that pigs can easily find their way through mazes that prove too difficult for many other animals.

Pigs won't stuff themselves silly.

Pigs will eat almost anything — even snow! But that doesn't mean pigs go hog wild over food. Unlike cows and horses, which will eat until they are ill, pigs stop when they feel full. After they have eaten, they usually nap until the next meal. Even without snacking between breakfast and dinner, pigs grow very quickly!

Answers to "When Pigs Fly": 1. e 2. a 3. f 4. b 5. c 6. d

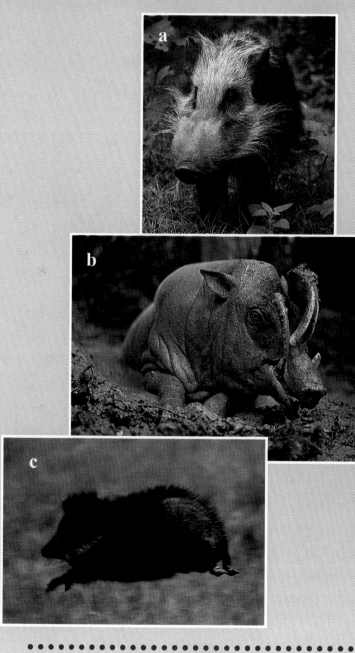

Picks of the Litter

Whether you're in Africa or Asia or somewhere in South America, you'll find a wild pig cousin or two! The **bush pig (a)** lives in the grasslands of Africa and Madagascar. Like a wart hog (another African wild pig), male bush pigs have warts on their faces. These warts help protect their faces from the tusks of other bush pigs when they fight. The **babirusa (b)** makes its home in southeast Asia. Its teeth, which can be longer than your foot, grow through the roof of its mouth and out the top of its snout. The **collared peccary (c)**, from South and Central America, is a more distant pig relation. A peccary will "woof" like a dog when its enemy the jaguar is nearby.

Pigs look dirty but really they're cool.

If you visit a farm, you'll probably find pigs covered with dried, caked mud. But it's not because pigs want to be dirty. They need the moisture found in mud. Pigs are very sensitive to heat but have no sweat glands to help them cool off. A coating of mud lowers their body temperature and stops sunburn. If there's clean water nearby, pigs will use that, too.

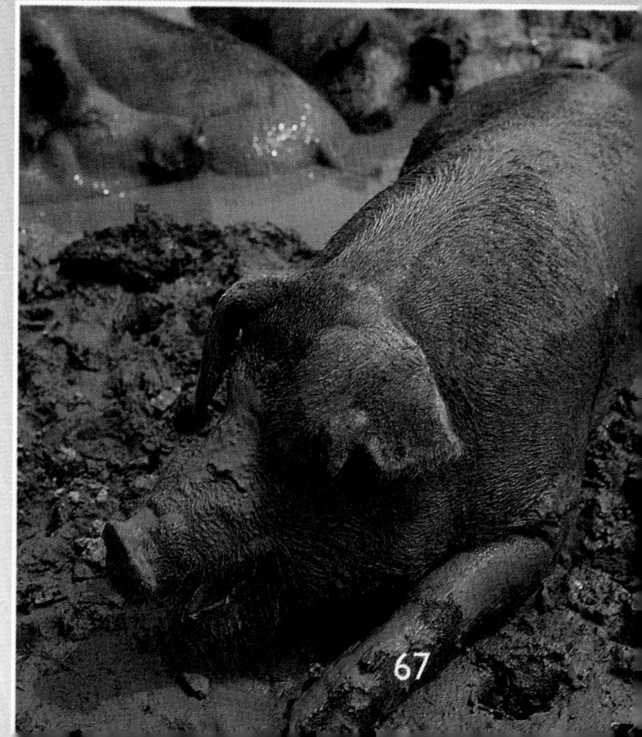

MEET THE AUTHOR

SUSAN LOWELL has some wild neighbors who often come over for a cactus dinner. That's because she lives in the Arizona desert, and her neighbors are piglike animals called *javelinas* (ha-ve-LEE-nas). The javelinas like to eat the thorny stems of the cactuses that grow near her ranch. Lowell enjoys watching the javelinas so much that she made up a story about them.

MEET THE ILLUSTRATOR

JIM HARRIS lives in Colorado on the side of a flat-topped mountain called a *mesa.* Every night, he can hear coyotes howling outside. Sometimes he even sees an elk walk across the deck outside his art studio. Harris has been drawing and painting since he was four years old.

THE THREE LITTLE JAVELINAS

by Susan Lowell

Illustrated by Jim Harris

ONCE UPON A TIME, way out in the desert, there were three little javelinas. Javelinas (ha-ve-LEE-nas) are wild, hairy, southwestern cousins of pigs.

Their heads were hairy, their backs were hairy, and their bony legs — all the way down to their hard little hooves — were very hairy. But their snouts were soft and pink.

One day, the three little javelinas trotted away to seek their fortunes. In this hot, dry land, the sky was almost always blue. Steep purple mountains looked down on the desert, where the cactus forests grew.

Soon the little javelinas came to a spot where the path divided, and each one went a different way.

The first little javelina wandered lazily along. He didn't see a dust storm whirling across the desert — until it caught him.

The whirlwind blew away and left the first little javelina sitting in a heap of tumbleweeds. Brushing himself off, he said, "I'll build a house with them!" And in no time at all, he did.

Then along came a coyote. He ran through the desert so quickly and so quietly that he was almost invisible. In fact, this was only one of Coyote's many magical tricks. He laughed when he saw the tumbleweed house and smelled the javelina inside.

"Mmm! A tender juicy piggy!" he thought. Coyote was tired of eating mice and rabbits.

He called out sweetly, "Little pig, little pig, let me come in."

"Not by the hair of my chinny-chin-chin!" shouted the first javelina (who had a lot of hair on his chinny-chin-chin!).

"Then I'll huff, and I'll puff, and I'll blow your house in!" said Coyote.

And he huffed, and he puffed, and he blew the little tumbleweed house away.

But in all the hullabaloo, the first little javelina escaped — and went looking for his brother and sister.

Coyote, who was very sneaky, tiptoed along behind.

The second little javelina walked for miles among giant cactus plants called saguaros (sa-WA-ros). They held their ripe red fruit high in the sky. But they made almost no shade, and the little javelina grew hot.

Then he came upon a Native American woman who was gathering sticks from inside a dried-up cactus. She planned to use these long sticks, called saguaro ribs, to knock down the sweet cactus fruit.

The second little javelina said, "Please, may I have some sticks to build a house?"

"Ha'u," (how) she said, which means "yes" in the language of the Desert People.

When he was finished building his house, he lay down in the shade. Then his brother arrived, panting from the heat, and the second little javelina moved over and made a place for him.

Pretty soon, Coyote found the saguaro rib house. He used his magic to make his voice sound just like another javelina's.

"Little pig, little pig, let me come in!" he called.

But the little javelinas were suspicious. The second one cried, "No! Not by the hair of my chinny-chin-chin!"

"Bah!" thought Coyote. "I am not going to eat your ***hair***."

Then Coyote smiled, showing all his sharp teeth: "I'll huff, and I'll puff, and I'll blow your house in!"

So he huffed, and he puffed, and all the saguaro ribs came tumbling down.

But the two little javelinas escaped into the desert.

Still not discouraged, Coyote followed. Sometimes his magic did fail, but then he usually came up with another trick.

The third little javelina trotted through beautiful palo verde trees, with green trunks and yellow flowers. She saw a snake sliding by, smooth as oil. A hawk floated round and round above her. Then she came to a place where a man was making adobe (a-DOE-be) bricks from mud and straw. The bricks lay on the ground, baking in the hot sun.

The third little javelina thought for a moment, and said, "May I please have a few adobes to build a house?"

"*Sí,*" answered the man, which means "yes" in Spanish, the brick-maker's language.

So the third javelina built herself a solid little adobe house, cool in summer and warm in winter. When her brothers found her, she welcomed them in and locked the door behind them.

Coyote followed their trail.

"Little pig, little pig, let me come in!" he called.

The three little javelinas looked out the window. This time Coyote pretended to be very old and weak, with no teeth and a sore paw. But they were not fooled.

"No! Not by the hair of my chinny-chin-chin," called back the third little javelina.

"Then I'll huff, and I'll puff, and I'll blow your house in!" said Coyote. He grinned, thinking of the wild pig dinner to come.

"Just try it!" shouted the third little javelina. So Coyote huffed and puffed, but the adobe bricks did not budge.

Again, Coyote tried. "I'll HUFF ... AND I'LL PUFF ... AND I'LL BLOW YOUR HOUSE IN!"

The three little javelinas covered their hairy ears. But nothing happened. The javelinas peeked out the window.

The tip of Coyote's raggedy tail whisked right past their noses. He was climbing upon the tin roof. Next, Coyote used his magic to make himself very skinny.

"The stove pipe!" gasped the third little javelina. Quickly she lighted a fire inside her wood stove.

"What a feast it will be!" Coyote said to himself. He squeezed into the stove pipe. "I think I'll eat them with red hot chile sauce!"

Whoosh. S-s-sizzle!

Then the three little javelinas heard an amazing noise. It was not a bark. It was not a cackle. It was not a howl. It was not a scream. It was all of those sounds together.

"Yip

yap

yeep

YEE-OWW-OOOOOOOOOOOOOO!"

Away ran a puff of smoke shaped like a coyote.

The three little javelinas lived happily ever after in the adobe house.

And if you ever hear a Coyote's voice, way out in the desert at night . . . well, you know what he's remembering!

RESPONDING

Something to *Howl* About

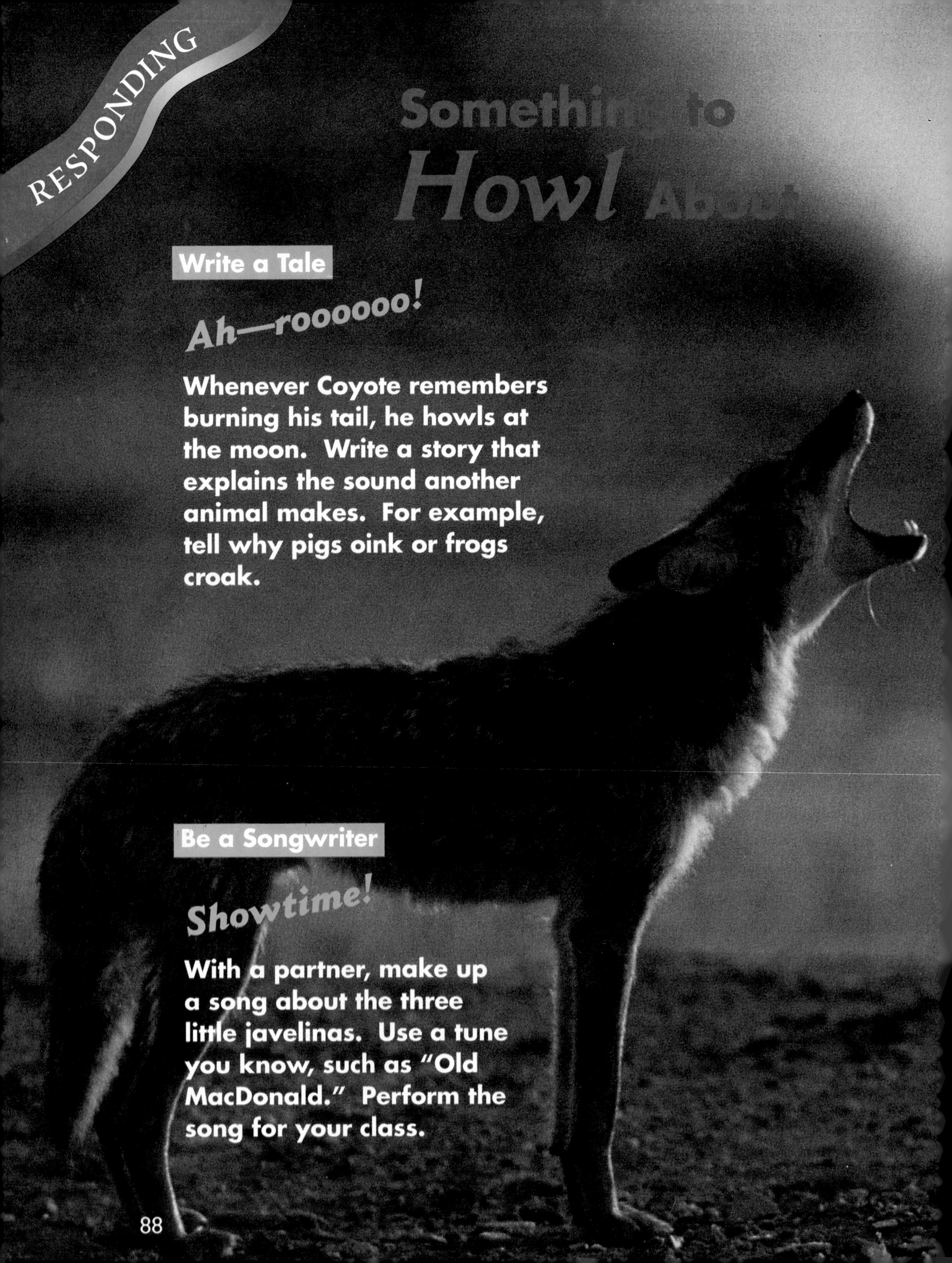

Write a Tale

Ah—roooooo!

Whenever Coyote remembers burning his tail, he howls at the moon. Write a story that explains the sound another animal makes. For example, tell why pigs oink or frogs croak.

Be a Songwriter

Showtime!

With a partner, make up a song about the three little javelinas. Use a tune you know, such as "Old MacDonald." Perform the song for your class.

My Hairy Neighbors

Meet some piglike animals that "talk" with stinky smells!

by Susan Lowell

photos by Thomas A. Wiewandt

Check out the rings of light hair around the necks of these peccaries. They look like collars, don't they? That's why the animals are called *collared peccaries*.

Welcome to my ranch. I live deep in a rocky canyon way out in the Arizona desert. I have many wild neighbors. At the end of a summer day, three of my favorites often come for dinner. Just watch!

There — a hairy animal is peeking through the bushes. And another. And another. It's Juan, José, and Josefina!

The animals are each about 20 inches (50 cm) high, with rounded backs. And they look and act a bit like pigs. But they're *peccaries* (PECK-a-rees). Some people around here also call them *javelinas* (ha-ve-LEE-nas).

A peccary can use its long, sharp teeth to bite a prickly pear cactus. Those teeth may look nasty, but this animal is probably just yawning.

Peccaries live in groups called *herds*, which helps them protect each other from their enemies. And when it's snooze time, the herd snuggles close together.

Peccaries often kneel to dig for food. See this one's knees? It has thick pads of skin there from kneeling so much!

A drippy hole on the javelina's back oozes a smelly liquid called *musk*. Family members rub the musk on each other. That helps them keep track of each other.

Peccary herds stick close together. This young one found a safe place in its herd — right in the thick of things.

Peccaries don't live just in deserts. In Mexico and much of South America, they also can be found in mountains and rain forests. They live only in wild areas. But some of those wild areas are very close to the homes of people.

As I go into my house, I suddenly hear some loud noise. *Clang! Bang! Clatter!*

What's that? Uh-oh! Outside my ranch house, Josefina just knocked over one of the trash cans. Her babies poke their snouts inside it and sniff for something good to eat.

"Shoo!" I say. "No junk food! Go find some nice cactus fruit." Josefina grunts. Together the herd starts moving. "Good night!" I call to them. Then I watch the herd gallop off into the desert darkness.

About the Author

Donivee Martin Laird

The beautiful state of Hawaii is home to Donivee Martin Laird. She was born there and lives there today with her family and a mongoose named Custard. Laird has written several Hawaiian versions of popular tales, such as *Wili Wai Kula and the Three Mongooses*, a Hawaiian "Goldilocks and the Three Bears."

About the Illustrator

Don Stuart

Don Stuart didn't have any brothers or sisters growing up, so he used to entertain himself by drawing. Making his own comic books was a favorite thing to do. Among the illustrators Stuart admires today is Lane Smith, the illustrator of *The True Story of the 3 Little Pigs*.

The Three Little Hawaiian Pigs and the Magic Shark

One morning in Hawaii a mother and father pig called their children together.

"Our dear pua'a keikis," they said with sorrow in their voices. "As much as we love you, it is time for you to become grown-ups and seek your own way in the

pua'a (poo AH ah) a Hawaiian word meaning pig

keiki (kay EE kee) what Hawaiians call a child

aloha (ah LOH ha) a Hawaiian word with meanings such as hello, goodbye, and love

world. Here is a sack of money for each of you. Spend it wisely and always be careful of strangers."

After saying aloha to their parents, the three little pigs set off down the road looking forward to a life full of happiness, adventure, and riches.

pili (PEE lee) **grass** a grass used to thatch grass houses in old Hawaii

opihi (oh PEE hee) a shallow, cone-shaped limpet shell whose animal is prized eating

They had gone only a short distance when they met a man with a load of pili grass. "Ah ha," said the first little pig. "This is for me. I will build myself a grass house and live beside the sea."

So, he bought the pili grass and happily headed towards the beach where he built his house. It was finished quickly and he took his pole, his net, his small bucket for opihi, and he went fishing.

The other two little pigs went on until they met a man selling driftwood. "Ah ha," said the second little pig. "This is for me. I will build myself a house of driftwood and live beside the sea."

Feeling pleased with himself, he quickly built his house and went to join the first little pig fishing and scraping opihi off the slippery rocks.

lava rock formed by a volcano

pau (POW) finished, all done

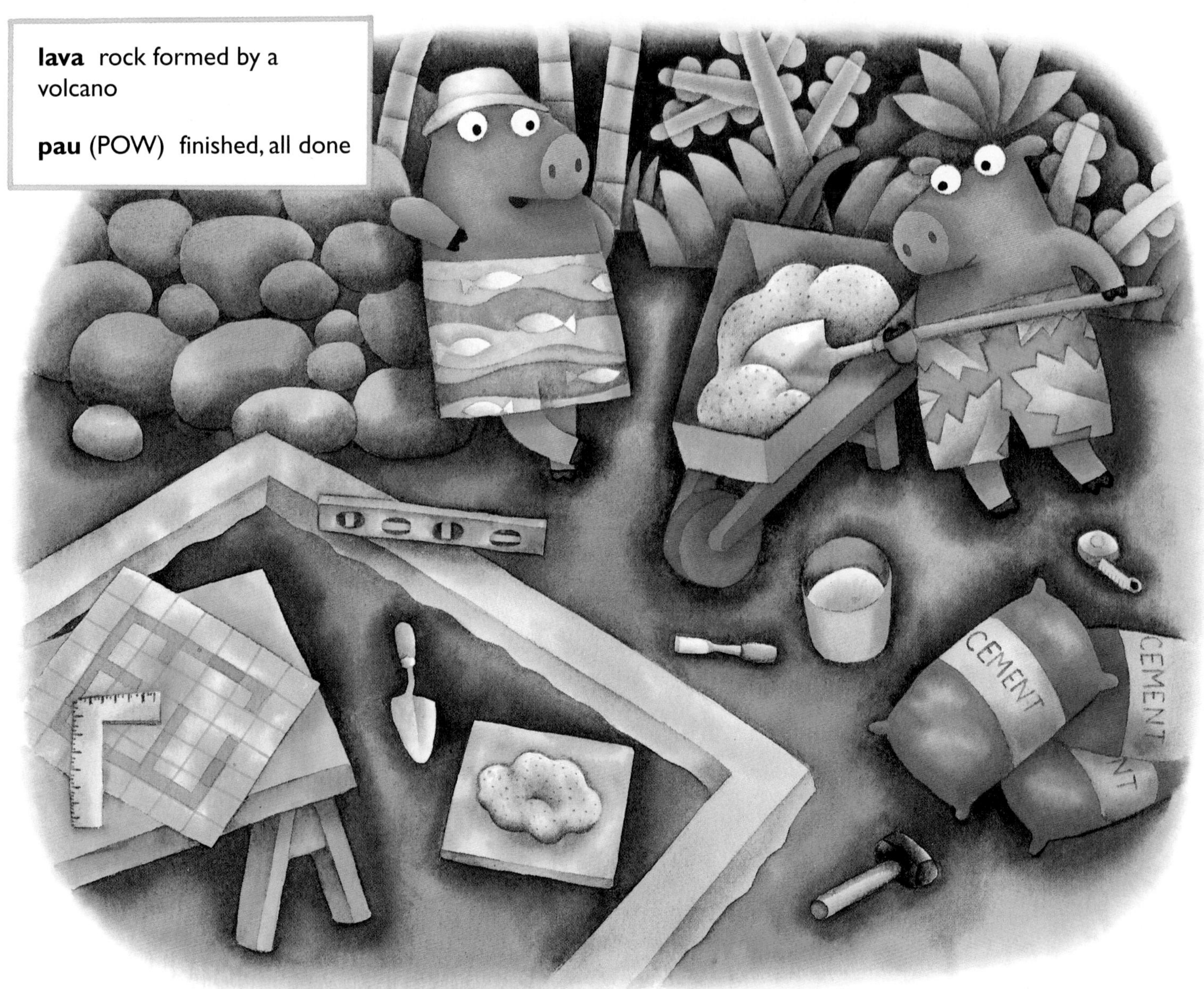

The third little pig went on until he met a man selling lava rock. "Ah ha," said the third little pig. "This is for me. I will build myself a house of lava rock and live beside the sea and go fishing with my brothers."

It took many days to build the house and before it was done, one brother came to visit the third little pig.

"Why are you wasting your time on such a hard house to build?" he asked. "We are pau with our houses and have time to fish and take it easy surfing and playing. Forget this house, come with us."

The third little pig just shook his head and said he would rather take his time and build a strong house.

After many days of hard work, the lava rock house was finished. It was sturdy and strong and the third little pig was pleased with his work. He checked his doors and windows carefully to be sure his house was snug and safe.

Then off he went to join his brothers beside the sea.

yellow tang a small bright yellow reef fish

humuhumu (hoo moo HOO moo) a member of the trigger fish family; one of whom is the humuhumu-nukunuku-a-pua‘a or fish with a snout like a pig, made famous in a popular Hawaiian song

he‘e (HAY ay) the Hawaiian word for octopus

puhi paka (POOK hee PAH kah) a ferocious eel with sharp teeth

The three little pigs threw their nets and pulled in reef creatures like the brilliant yellow tang, the horned humuhumu, or the slimy octopus, he‘e. They climbed over the wet rocks scraping off the delicious opihi and once in a while they caught puhi paka, the fierce fanged eel.

ulua (oo LOO ah) a kind of crevalle or jack fish

opakapaka (oh pah kah PAH kah) a blue snapper fish

ahi (AH hee) a yellow fin tuna fish

trade winds breezes which keep Hawaii cool

Sometimes they took their poles, and standing far out on the rocks, fished the deeper waters for the larger ulua, opakapaka, and ahi. They played tag, splashed in the tide pools, and chased tiny sand crabs. Their days were clear and sunny, and cooled by gentle trade winds.

When the waves broke just right beside the reef, they took their surfboards and caught long breathtaking rides to the beach.

Meanwhile, an evil magic shark watched them from deep down where the water is green. Back and forth swam the magic shark, his long teeth shining in the gloomy water. He especially wanted to eat the three little pigs since they looked so sweet and tender.

He knew he couldn't catch them on the rocks, for the lava was sharp and the pigs too quick. He wished they would fall off their surfboards, but the pigs were too good and went too fast through the rough water.

So, watching and planning, the magic shark drooled and thought of the yummy little pigs.

shave ice powdery ice shavings put in a paper cone and covered with sweet, flavored syrup

One morning, unable to stand his craving any longer, the magic shark disguised himself as a shave ice man and knocked on the door of the first little pig's house. "Little Pig, Little Pig, let me come in," he called. "I have plenty shave ice!"

The little pig peeked out of the window. He was hot and thirsty and the cool, colorful shave ice looked so tasty. He grabbed his money and started to open the door.

But, just in time, he saw a fin on the shave ice man's back and he knew it was really the magic shark. He quickly shut and locked the door.

The shark knocked harder and called, "Little Pig, Little Pig, let me come in."

"Oh no," cried the little pig. "Not by the hair on my chinny, chin, chin."

The magic shark was hot and hungry and the little pig's answer made him very mad. He yelled, "Little Pig, Little Pig, let me come in or I will huff and I will puff and I will blow your house down."

The little pig did not open his door. (After all he wasn't crazy, he knew what the magic shark wanted.)

So, the very mad magic shark huffed and the very mad magic shark puffed and the very mad magic shark blew down the first little pig's house.

The first little pig ran out of the back door and down the path to the house of the second little pig. The very mad magic shark went back to the ocean to cool off and make a new plan.

lei (LAY) a garland (usually of flowers)

ukulele (oo koo LAY lay) a four-stringed instrument played by strumming, 'uke' is short for ukulele

nose flute a flute like instrument played by blowing air with the nose

In a few days, the magic shark was hungry for little pigs again. This time he dressed up as a beachboy, wearing white pants, a coconut leaf hat, and a lei around his neck. He knocked on the door of the second little pig's house and called, "Little Pig, Little Pig, let's talk story and play ukes."

The little pigs grabbed their ukulele and nose flute and opened the door. The beachboy smiled and the little pigs saw rows and rows of long, sharp white teeth and just in time, they slammed the door.

"Little Pig, Little Pig, let me come in," called the hot and hungry magic shark anxiously.

"Oh no," cried the little pigs. (They knew that was no friendly beachboy out on the steps.) "Not by the hairs on our chinny, chin, chins."

This made the magic shark upset so he roared, "Then I will huff and I will puff and I will blow your house down." Just as he said he would, the very upset magic shark huffed and the very upset magic shark puffed and the very upset magic shark blew down the house of the second little pig.

The little pig and his brother jumped out of the window and ran down the path to the house of the third little pig.

mu'u mu'u (MOO oo MOO oo) a long, loose fitting woman's dress

lauhala (loo HAH lah) leaf of the hala or Pandanus tree; used in weaving hats, rugs, and baskets

Once more the magic shark, hot and still hungry, swam angrily down to his watery home to plot and scheme. After a few days his hunger pangs were so bad that the magic shark decided to try again.

This time he went pretending to be a lei seller. He knocked on the third little pig's door and called sweetly, "Little Pig, Little Pig, let me come in. I have leis to sell."

The three little pigs loved to wear leis and were happy to hear a sweet voice calling.

They looked out and saw the lei seller in her mu'u mu'u and lauhala hat, with flower leis on her arms. But then, they also saw a shark's tail sticking out from under the mu'u mu'u. They knew who that was so they rushed around locking the doors and windows.

"Little Pig, Little Pig, let me come in," called the magic shark, growing upset.

"Oh no," answered the little pigs. "Not by the hairs on our chinny, chin, chins."

"You will be sorry!" screamed the furious magic shark in his loudest voice. "I will huff and I will puff and I will blow your house down." No one answered and no one opened the door, so the furious magic shark huffed and the furious magic shark puffed and he huffed and he puffed and he blew . . . and nothing happened!

Again he huffed and he puffed and he huffed and he puffed and he blew and he blew and still nothing happened.

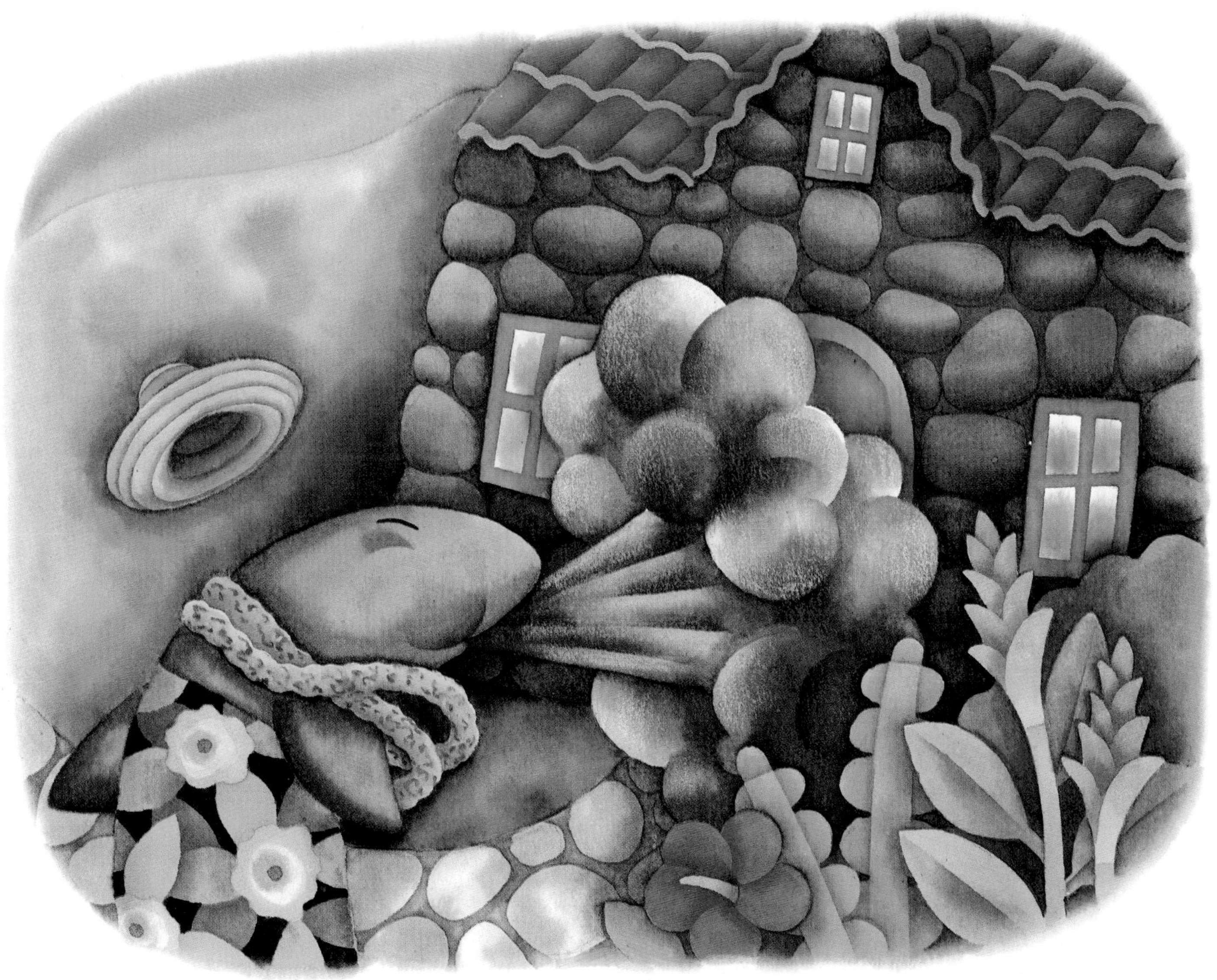

Once more the furious magic shark huffed and the furious magic shark puffed and the furious magic shark huffed and the furious magic shark puffed and the furious magic shark blew and blew and still . . . the lava rock house stood firm.

Now this made the magic shark extremely furious. So, gathering up all of his air, the extremely furious magic shark huffed and puffed and huffed and puffed and huffed and puffed

and blew
and blew
and blew
and blew
and blew
and blew
and blew

until . . . whoosh; ker-splat, he fell on the ground all out of air looking like a flat balloon!

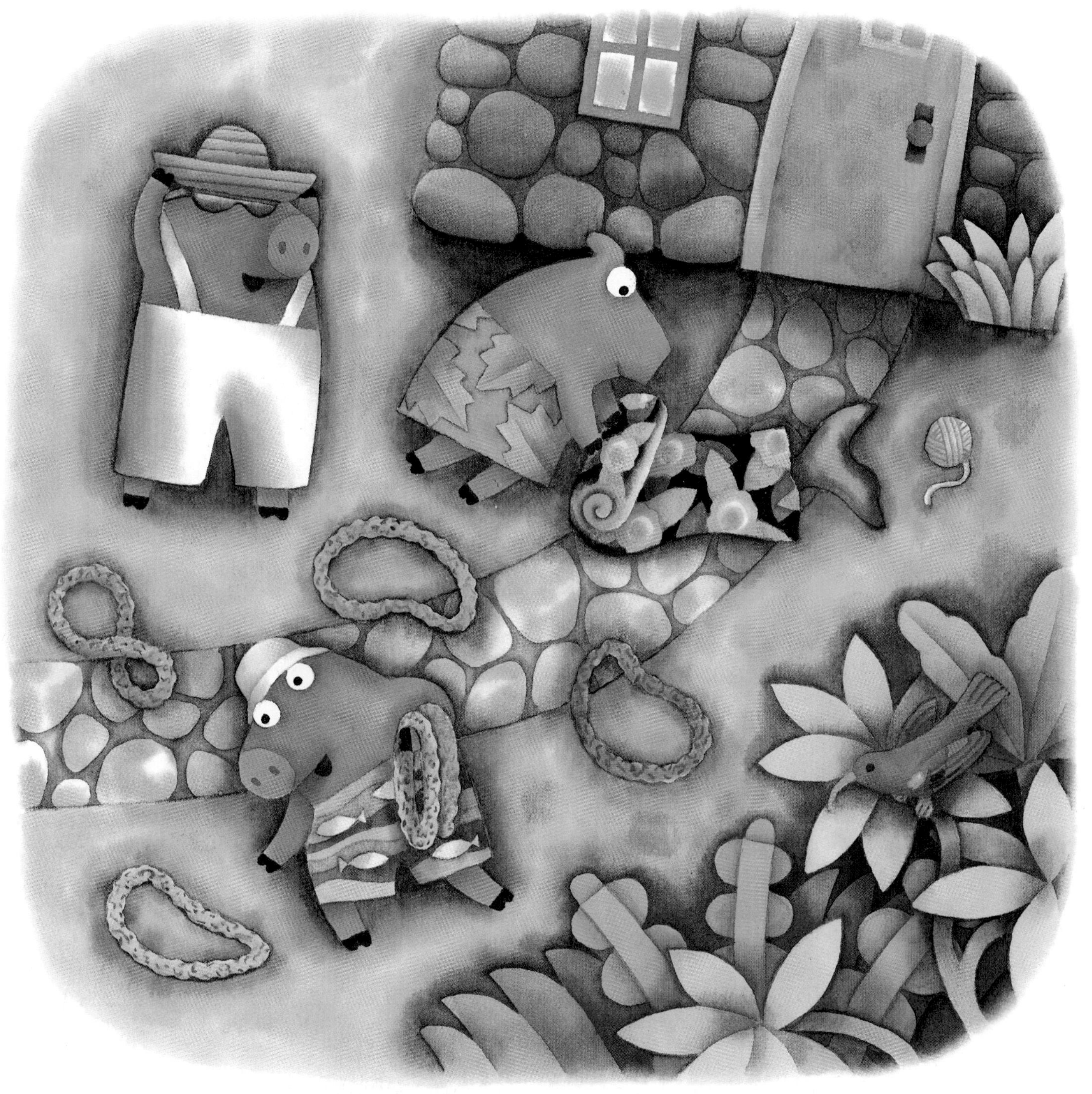

It was quiet and still and the three little pigs cautiously peeked out of the house. Seeing the very flat magic shark, they quickly ran outside, rolled him up like a straw mat, and tied a string around him.

Then . . . taking him off to the dump they threw him away.

When they returned to the seashore, the third little pig helped his brothers build sturdy rock houses and once they were finished, the three little pigs gave a large party. They invited all their friends and relatives as well as a shave ice man (without a fin) to serve

refreshments, a beachboy (without rows of sharp white teeth) to join the musicians, and a lei seller (without a shark's tail) to give out leis.

From then on the three little pigs lived safely and peacefully beside the sea.

RESPONDING

Aloha, Little Pigs

Write a Paragraph

Dear Magic Shark

The shark didn't have much luck fooling the pigs. Can you think of a better disguise he could have used? Write a paragraph to give the shark advice on what to wear and how to act.

Act Out a Scene

Let Me Come In!

With a group of friends, act out your favorite scene from the story. You'll need one person to play each part and another to be the narrator. It might be fun to make props to help you tell the story.

Pigs

by
Charles Ghigna

Pigs are playful
Pigs are pink
Pigs are smarter
Than you think

Pigs are slippery
Pigs are stout
Pigs have noses
Called a snout

Pigs are pudgy
Pigs are plump
Pigs can run
But never jump

Pigs are loyal
Pigs are true
Pigs don't care for
Barbecue

Surprise, Surprise

A story by Kara Johnson

Mr. Pig has a surprise in store for him! Read what happens on his special day.

Surprise, Surprise

It was a sunny day. The birds were singing, the trees and shrubs in full bloom, but Whooper City was a state of confusion. The streets were packed with people bustling all around.

Mr. Reindeer, the Whooper City mail carrier, had a very important letter for Mr. Pig. He could hear the shower running inside Mr. Pig's house. "Mr. Pig, Mr. Pig!" he screamed at the top of his lungs. Mr. Reindeer had a party to go to, so he was finishing his job as fast as possible. Finally, Mr. Pig came out in a towel and got the morning's mail.

A moment later Mr. Pig came down specially dressed because it was his birthday. He sifted through the mail, hoping to find a birthday card, but all he could find was a notice for a meeting at Ms. Rabbit's house. It read:

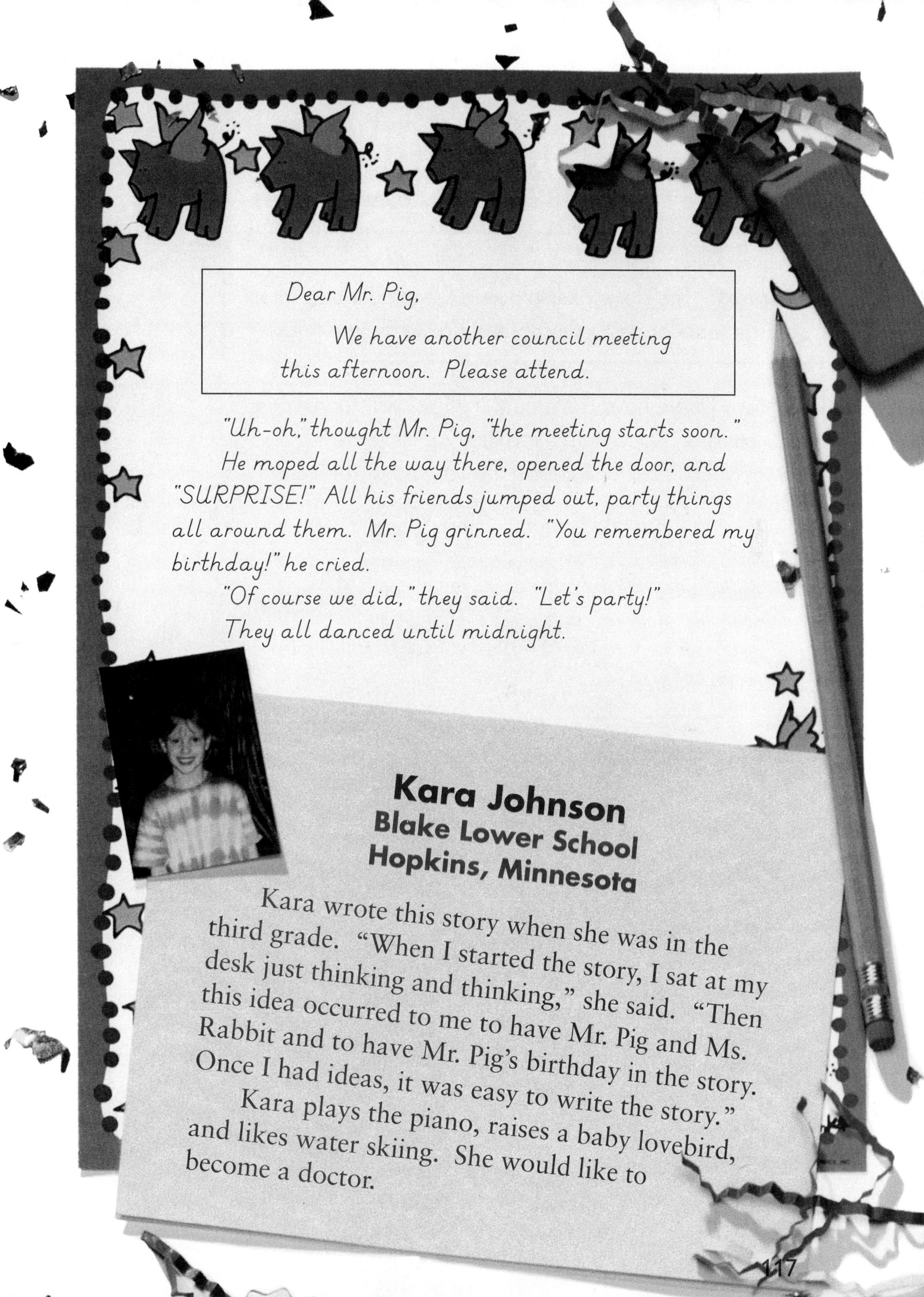

Dear Mr. Pig,

We have another council meeting this afternoon. Please attend.

"Uh-oh," thought Mr. Pig, "the meeting starts soon." He moped all the way there, opened the door, and "SURPRISE!" All his friends jumped out, party things all around them. Mr. Pig grinned. "You remembered my birthday!" he cried.

"Of course we did," they said. "Let's party!"

They all danced until midnight.

Kara Johnson

Blake Lower School
Hopkins, Minnesota

Kara wrote this story when she was in the third grade. "When I started the story, I sat at my desk just thinking and thinking," she said. "Then this idea occurred to me to have Mr. Pig and Ms. Rabbit and to have Mr. Pig's birthday in the story. Once I had ideas, it was easy to write the story."

Kara plays the piano, raises a baby lovebird, and likes water skiing. She would like to become a doctor.

The Wild Boar & the Fox

An Aesop's Fable retold by Dr. Albert Cullum

Characters: Boar, Fox
Staging: The story takes place in the middle of a forest. A large table or desk can represent a sturdy tree trunk.

Boar: Now that I have a moment, I think I will sharpen my teeth. Here is a nice sturdy tree that will help me. *(Rubs and rubs his tusks against the very hard tree trunk.)*

Fox: What in the world are you doing, Boar?

Boar: I'm sharpening my tusks.

Fox: That seems like a very silly thing to be doing.

Boar: Really! Why?

Fox: It's silly, for I don't see any danger about. I don't see a hunter and his dogs coming after you!

Boar: I don't see a hunter and his dogs coming after me, either.

Fox: Well, then, why all the nonsense about sharpening your tusks?

Boar: Fox, I don't think you understand. Wouldn't it be foolish of me to wait until the hunter and his dogs attacked before I sharpened my tusks? I think you are silly, not me!

Moral:

Think ahead and be prepared.

Community Ties

Contents

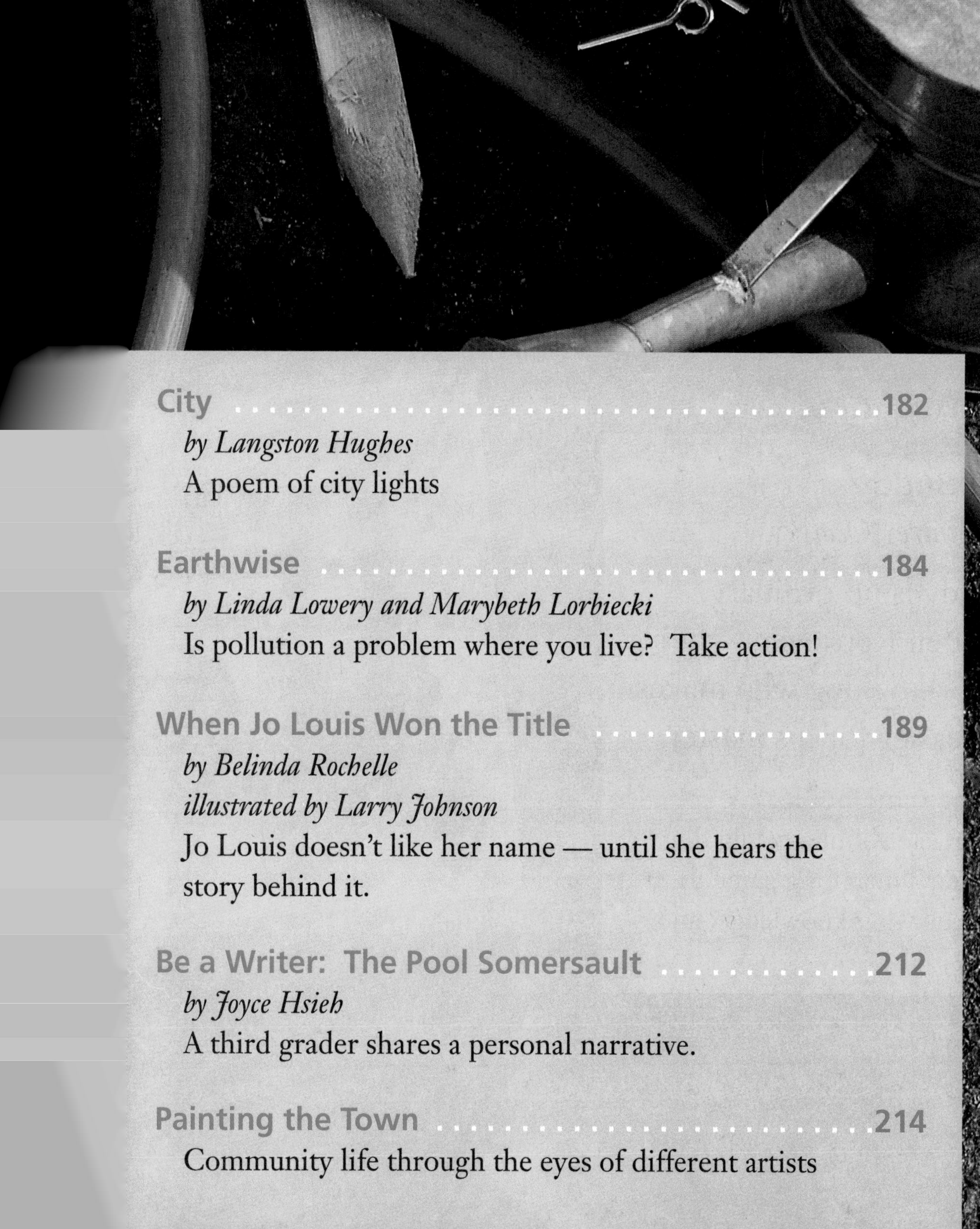

Read On Your Own

PAPERBACK **PLUS**

My Buddy

by Audrey Osofsky

Buddy is no ordinary Golden Retriever — he's a working dog who makes life easier for his master.

In the same book . . .
An article about a young dog trainer, a matching game to test your dog knowledge, and more

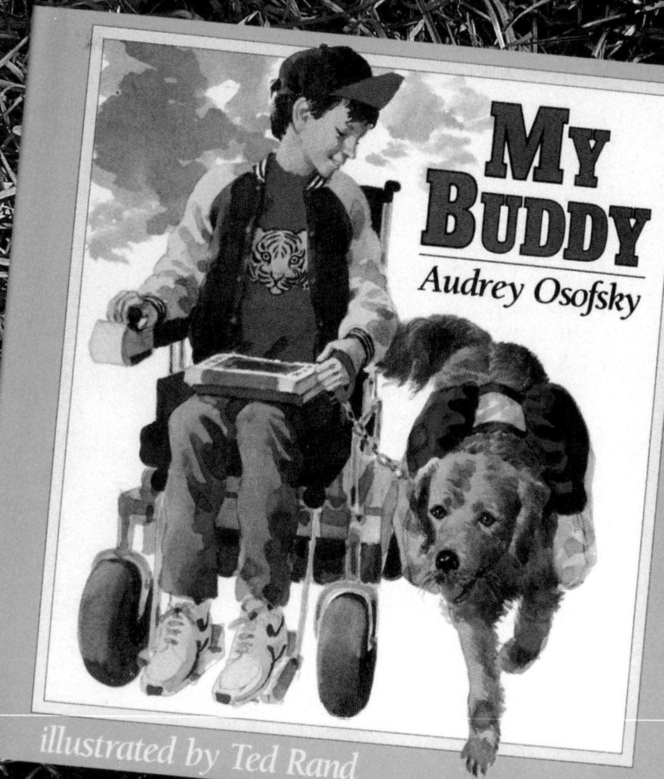

PAPERBACK **PLUS**

Cam Jansen and the Mystery of the Babe Ruth Baseball

by David A. Adler

Cam Jansen covers all the bases in her search for a stolen baseball signed by the Babe.

In the same book . . .
More about baseball, including statistics and card-collecting tips

Stories from Around Town

Tar Beach

by Faith Ringgold

Dreams come true on a magical summer night in New York City.

Pearl Moscowitz's Last Stand

by Arthur Levine

Mrs. Moscowitz takes on City Hall to save the gingko trees in her neighborhood.

Vejigante Masquerader

by Lulu Delacre

Will Ramón finish his costume in time for the annual carnival?

Eskimo Boy: Life in an Inupiaq Eskimo Village

by Russ Kendall

An Eskimo boy takes you on a tour of his Alaskan village.

About the Author

Roni Schotter doesn't have to look far for story ideas. When she lived in New York City, she saw many fruit and vegetable stands in the streets. The fruits and vegetables were as colorful to look at as they were good to eat. That's what inspired her to write *A Fruit & Vegetable Man*.

About the Illustrator

Jeanette Winter likes to draw. Sometimes she likes to write. And sometimes she likes to do both, as she did in the book *Follow the Drinking Gourd*. In her spare time, when she's not drawing or writing, Winter enjoys taking photographs.

A Fruit & Vegetable Man

by Roni Schotter
Pictures by Jeanette Winter

Ruby Rubenstein was a fruit and vegetable man. His motto was "I take care." Six mornings a week, long before the sun was up, Ruby was.

"*Is it time,* Ruby?" his wife Trudy always asked from deep under the covers.

"It's time," Ruby always answered. Then he'd jump out of bed, touch his knees, then his toes, and hurry uptown to market to choose the ripest fruit and vegetables for his store.

For nearly fifty years it had been so — ever since he and Trudy first sailed across the ocean to make a new life together.

Every morning before school, Sun Ho and his sister, Young Mee, who with their family, had just flown across the sky to make a new life together, came to watch Ruby work his magic.

"Yo-ho, Mr. Ruby!" Sun Ho would call out. "Show me!"

And nodding to Sun Ho, Ruby would pile apples, tangerines, and pears in perfect pyramids, arrange grapes in diamonds, insert a head of lettuce as accent, then tuck in a bunch of broccoli or a bit of watercress for trim.

It was like seeing a great artist at work. Sun Ho felt honored to be there. "Like a painting, Mr. Ruby!" he would say shyly.

Ruby always smiled, and his smile filled Sun Ho with happiness and, deep inside, a strange feeling that was like wishing. Sun Ho watched as Ruby juggled cantaloupes, then cut them into wedges and packed them neatly in plastic. Inside Sun Ho, the feeling that was like wishing grew stronger.

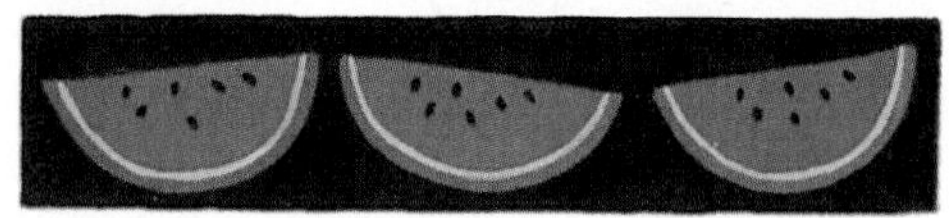

.19
JUICY
79¢
PEARS
89¢
49

"He's an artist, all right," Old Ella from up the block always said, pocketing an apple and a handful of prunes.

Ruby didn't mind. He'd just wink and utter one wonderful word: "Taste!" Then he'd offer whatever he had on special that day to Sun Ho, his sister, and anyone who wanted.

"What would we *do* without Ruby?" Mary Morrissey asked the crowd one gray afternoon. The people of Delano Street sighed and shook their heads at such a terrible thought.

"Mr. Ruby," Sun Ho said, "he's one of a kind."

Yes, everyone on Delano Street appreciated Ruby. But Ruby was getting old. Lately, when he got up to

touch his knees and his toes, there was a stiffness Ruby pretended he didn't feel and a creaking Trudy pretended she didn't hear. And sometimes, though Ruby never would admit it, there was a wish that he could stay a little longer in bed with Trudy.

"Ruby," Trudy said to him one morning from under the covers. "Long ago you and I made a promise. We said if ever we got old, we'd sell the business and go to live in the mountains. *Is it time, Ruby?"*

"NO!!" Ruby thundered. And he leapt out of bed, did *twice* his usual number of exercises, and ran off to market.

As if to prove he was as young as ever, he worked especially hard at the store that day and made some of his most beautiful designs.

That afternoon, Sun Ho came by as Ruby was arranging potatoes in his own special way. Sun Ho watched as Ruby whirled them in the air and tossed them with such skill that they landed perfectly, one next to the other in a neat row.

"Yo-ho, Mr. Ruby!" Sun Ho said, filled with admiration. "Teach me?"

Proudly, Ruby grabbed an Idaho and two russets and taught Sun Ho how to juggle. Next he taught him how to pile grapefruits to keep them from falling. By the time Sun Ho's parents stopped by, Ruby had even taught Sun Ho how to work the register. Then he sat Sun Ho down and told him how, early every morning, he went to market to choose his fruit and vegetables.

EGGPLANT
69¢
$1.29
FRESH
79¢
SPANISH
59¢
POTAT

"Take me!" Sun Ho pleaded, the feeling that was like wishing so big now he felt he might burst. "Please?"

Ruby thought only for a moment. Then he spoke. "My pleasure," he announced.

So early the next day, while Venus still sparkled in the dark morning sky, Ruby took Sun Ho to market. Sun Ho

had an excellent nose, and together he and Ruby sniffed out the most fragrant fruit and sampled the choicest chicory. Then Ruby showed Sun Ho how he talked and teased and argued his way to the best prices.

All the rest of that long day, Sun Ho felt special. And Ruby? He felt, well . . . tired. Whenever Trudy was busy with a customer, Ruby leaned over and pretended to tie his shoe, but what he did, really, was *yawn*. By afternoon, Ruby was running out of the store every few minutes. "The fruit!" he'd yell to Trudy. "Got to fix the fruit!" he'd say, but once outside, what he did, really, was *sneeze*.

"To your health, Mr. Ruby," Sun Ho whispered, sneaking him a handkerchief.

"Thank you, Mr. Sun Ho," Ruby said, quietly blowing his nose.

That evening it began to snow on Delano Street. It snowed all night, and by morning the street was cold and white, the color of fresh cauliflower.

For the first time in many years, Ruby woke up feeling sick. His face was red, his forehead hot. "No work today," Trudy said. "Ruby's Fruit and Vegetable is closed until further notice." What would the people of Delano Street do without him? Ruby wondered. But he was too sick to care.

When Sun Ho arrived at the store that day and saw that it was closed, he was worried. Where was Ruby?

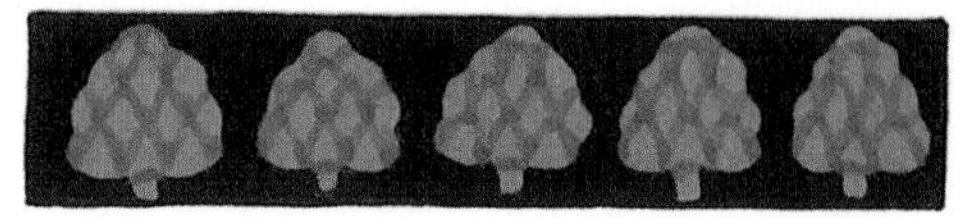

LMO
RUBY'S FRUIT & VEGETABLE
307
FRESH
DAILY
CLOSED
LAU
DROP
SERV
RU
FR
VEG

Upstairs in his bed, Ruby dozed, dreaming of spring and fresh apricots. Once, when he opened his eyes, Sun Ho was standing next to him . . . or was he?

"No worries," Sun Ho seemed to say. "I take care." Then as strangely as he had appeared, Sun Ho disappeared. Was Ruby dreaming?

For the next three days, for the first time in his life, Ruby was too sick to think or worry about his store. He

stayed deep under the covers, enjoying Trudy's loving care, and more than that, her barley soup. On the morning of the fourth day, he felt well enough to worry. On the morning of the fifth day, a Saturday, there was no stopping him. "My store!" he shouted. Leaning on Trudy's arm, he put on his clothes. Then he rushed off to reopen.

What a surprise when he arrived! The store was open. In fact, it looked as if it had never been shut. The peppers were in pyramids, the dates in diamonds, the winter tomatoes in triangles. Sun Ho's father was helping Old Ella to a pound of carrots. Sun Ho's mother was at the register. Young Mee was polishing pears. And, in the center of it all, Sun Ho stood smiling, offering customers a taste of something new — bean sprouts!

When they saw Ruby, everyone cheered. Ruby bowed with pleasure.

"I took care, Mr. Ruby!" Sun Ho called out proudly.

"I see," Ruby answered. "You're a fruit and vegetable man, Sun Ho, like me."

Sun Ho's face turned the color of Ruby's radishes. The feeling that was like wishing was gone now. In its place was a different feeling: pride.

SPECIAL
89¢
Bean Sprout
59¢
149

"Is it time, Ruby?" Trudy whispered.

Ruby sighed. He thought about how much he liked Sun Ho and his family and how carefully they had kept his store. He thought about the stiffness and creaking in his knees. He thought about the mountains and about Trudy's loving care. More than that, he thought about her barley soup.

"It's time," he said finally.

Now Sun Ho is a fruit and vegetable man! Every morning, long before the sun is up, long before it's time for school, Sun Ho and his family are up, ready to hurry to market to choose the ripest fruit and vegetables for their store.

And Ruby? He's still a fruit and vegetable man . . . only now he and Trudy grow their own.

Ideas to Pick From

Write a Letter

Dear Ruby, How Are You?

Write a letter to tell Ruby the news about his old store and neighborhood. What changes have been made? What things are still the same?

Finding Out About a Career

Learning on the Job

Sun Ho learned about running a store from an expert: Ruby. Find out about a job you'd like to have. Talk to someone who has that job, or read a book about it. Share what you learn.

EDISON BEAUTIFUL

photos by Fred Boyle

When the Thomas A. Edison Elementary School in Long Beach, California, needed sprucing up, more than 2,300 students, parents, teachers, and other volunteers got together with paintbrushes in hand.

Painting the flagpole in front of the school kept Jonny Keebler busy all day. "It was neat!" he said. "I was helping to work on a school to make it look better."

A total of 366 gallons of paint was used to give the school building a new look. On the wall surrounding the school, volunteers painted a mural designed by students. The mural is easy to spot from the off-ramp of the freeway.

People of all ages turned out for the two-day event, which was part of International Community Service Day. Local businesses donated most of the materials for the project, including eighty cypress trees and forty bushes.

After working hard, everyone was tired and ready to eat. Twenty-eight vanilla and chocolate sheet cakes were made into one enormous cake for the end-of-the-project celebration. Students at Edison Elementary couldn't wait to go to school on Monday!

Meet Carmen Lomas Garza

The pictures in this book are all painted from my memories of growing up in Kingsville, Texas, near the border with Mexico. From the time I was a young girl I always dreamed of becoming an artist. I practiced drawing every day; I studied art in school; and I finally did become an artist. My family has inspired and encouraged me for all these years. This is my book of family pictures.

Los cuadros de este libro los pinté de los recuerdos de mi niñez en Kingsville, Texas, cerca de la frontera con México. Desde que era pequeña, siempre soñé con ser artista. Dibujaba cada día; estudié arte en la escuela; y por fin, me hice artista. Mi familia me ha inspirado y alentado todos estos años. Éste es mi libro de cuadros de familia.

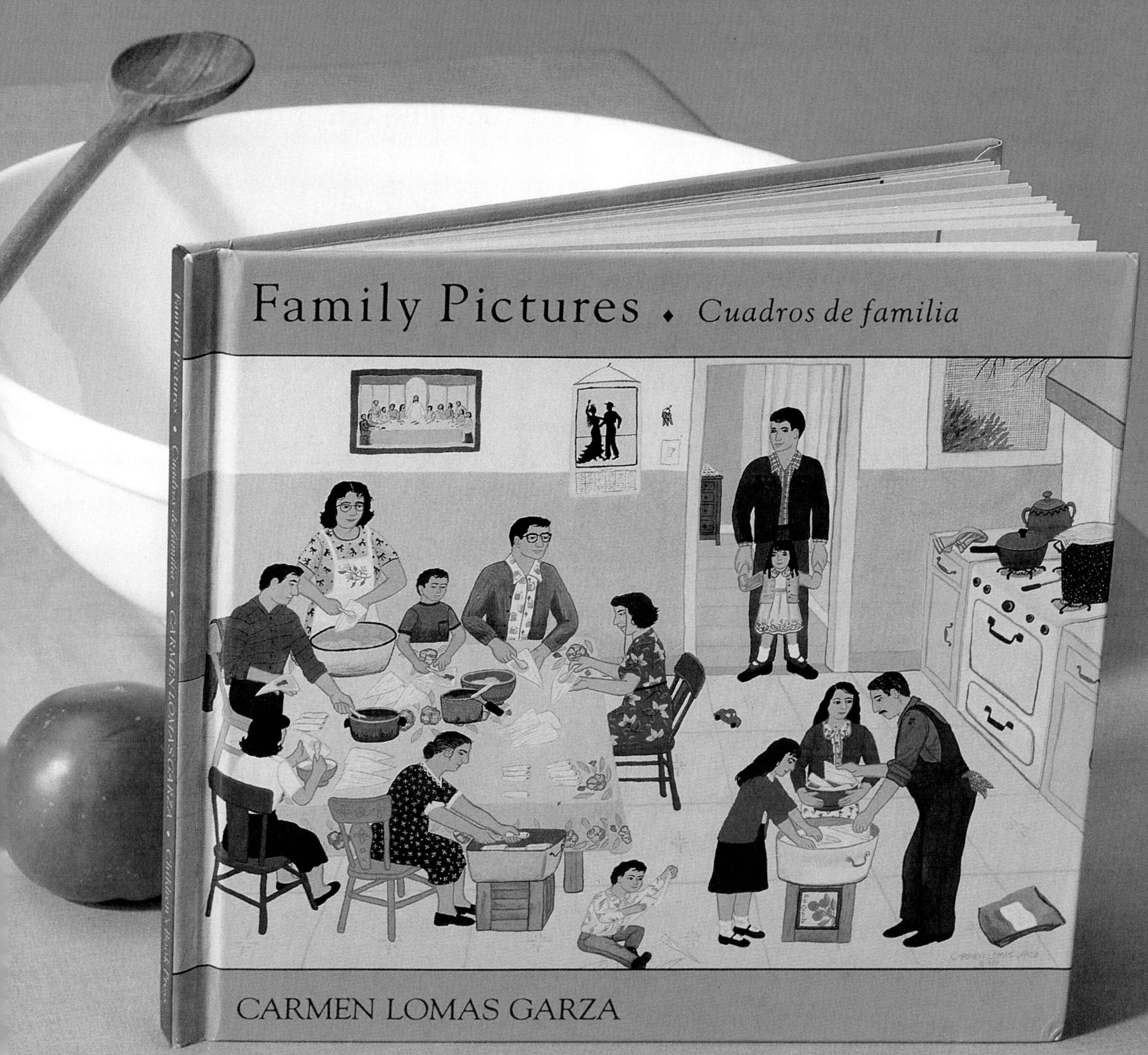
Family Pictures ◆ Cuadros de familia
CARMEN LOMAS GARZA

The Fair in Reynosa

My friends and I once went to a very big fair across the border in Reynosa, Mexico. The fair lasted a whole week. Artisans and entertainers came from all over Mexico. There were lots of booths with food and crafts. This is one little section where everybody is ordering and eating tacos.

I painted a father buying tacos and the rest of the family sitting down at the table. The little girl is the father's favorite and that's why she gets to tag along with him. I can always recognize little girls who are their fathers' favorites.

La Feria en Reynosa

Una vez, mis amigos y yo fuimos a una feria muy grande en Reynosa, México, al otro lado de la frontera. La feria duró una semana entera. Vinieron artesanos y artistas de todo México. Había muchos puestos que vendían comida y artesanías. Ésta es una pequeña parte de la feria donde todos están comprando tacos y comiéndoselos.

Pinté a un padre comprando tacos y al resto de la familia sentada a la mesa. La niñita pequeña es la preferida de su papá, y por eso es que él la permite acompañarlo. Aún hoy, siempre puedo reconocer cuando una niñita es la preferida de su papá.

SODAS
CocaCola
Fresa $5.00
Limon pesos
CARNE
ASADA
Con Tomate
y
Salsa $12.00
pesos
CARMEN LOMAS GARZA
©1987
La feria en Reynosa

Oranges

We were always going to my grandparents' house, so whatever they were involved in we would get involved in. In this picture my grandmother is hanging up the laundry. We told her that the oranges needed picking so she said, "Well, go ahead and pick some." Before she knew it, she had too many oranges to hold in her hands, so she made a basket out of her apron. That's my brother up in the tree, picking oranges. The rest of us are picking up the ones that he dropped on the ground.

Naranjas

Siempre íbamos a la casa de mis abuelos, así que cualquier cosa que estuvieran haciendo ellos, nosotros la hacíamos también. En este cuadro, mi abuela está colgando la ropa a secar. Nosotros le dijimos que las naranjas estaban listas para cosechar, y ella nos respondió: —Vayan pues, recójanlas. En un dos por tres, tenía demasiadas naranjas para sostenerlas en las manos, así que convirtió su delantal en canasta. Ése es mi hermano, en el árbol, recogiendo naranjas. El resto de nosotros estamos recogiendo las que él deja caer al suelo.

CARMEN LOMAS GARZA
©1988

For Dinner

This is my grandparents' backyard. My grandmother is killing a chicken for dinner. My grandfather is in the chicken coop trying to catch another chicken. Later, my family will sit down to eat Sunday dinner — chicken soup.

That's me in the blue dress with my younger brother, Arturo. He was so surprised by the scene that he started to spill his snowcone. We had never seen anything like that before. I knew my grandparents had always raised chickens, but I never knew how the chickens got to be soup.

Para la cena

Éste es el patio de mis abuelos. Mi abuela está matando a una gallina para la cena. Mi abuelo está en el gallinero tratando de atrapar a otra gallina. Más tarde, mi familia se sentará a comer la cena del domingo: sopa de pollo.

Ésa soy yo, vestida de azul, con mi hermano menor, Arturo. Él estaba tan sorprendido por lo que veía que se le empezó a derramar su raspa. Nunca antes habíamos visto algo parecido. Yo sabía que mis abuelos criaban gallinas, pero no había sabido antes cómo era que las gallinas se convertían en sopa.

CARMEN LOMA

Birthday Party

That's me hitting the piñata at my sixth birthday party. It was also my brother's fourth birthday. My mother made a big birthday party for us and invited all kinds of friends, cousins and neighborhood kids.

You can't see the piñata when you're trying to hit it, because your eyes are covered with a handkerchief. My father is pulling the rope that makes the piñata go up and down. He will make sure that everybody has a chance to hit it at least once. Somebody will end up breaking it, and that's when all the candies will fall out and all the kids will run and try to grab them.

Cumpleaños

Ésa soy yo, pegándole a la piñata en la fiesta que me dieron cuando cumplí seis años. Era también el cumpleaños de mi hermano, que cumplía cuatro años. Mi madre nos dio una gran fiesta e invitó a muchos primos, vecinos y amigos.

No puedes ver la piñata cuando le estás dando con el palo, porque tienes los ojos cubiertos por un pañuelo. Mi padre está tirando de la cuerda que sube y baja la piñata. Él se encargará de que todos tengan por lo menos una oportunidad de pegarle a la piñata. Luego alguien acabará rompiéndola, y entonces todos los caramelos que tiene dentro caerán y todos los niños correrán a cogerlos.

Cakewalk

Cakewalk was a game to raise money to send Mexican Americans to the university. You paid 25 cents to stand on a number. When the music started, you walked around and around. When the music stopped, whatever number you happened to step on was your number. Then one of the ladies in the center would pick out a number from the can. If you were standing on the winning number, you would win a cake. That's my mother in the center of the circle in the pink and black dress. My father is serving punch. I'm the little girl in front of the store scribbling on the sidewalk with a twig.

Cakewalk

Cakewalk era un juego que se hacía para recaudar fondos para darles becas universitarias a jóvenes méxico-americanos. Se pagaba 25 centavos para poder pararse sobre un número. Cuando la música empezaba a tocar, todos empezaban a caminar en círculo. Cuando se terminaba la música, el número sobre el cual estabas parado era tu número. Entonces una de las señoras que estaba en el centro del círculo escogía un número de la lata. Si estabas parado sobre el número de la suerte, ganabas un pastel. Ésa es mi madre en el centro del círculo, vestida de rosado y negro. Mi papá está sirviendo ponche. Yo soy la niñita dibujando garabatos en la acera al frente de la tienda con una ramita.

MATILDE'S GRO.
Yerbas Piñatas
OJAS
Rainbow Bread
Rainbow Bread
CAKEWALK

Picking Nopal Cactus

In the early spring my grandfather would come and get us and we'd all go out into the woods to pick nopal cactus. My grandfather and my mother are slicing off the fresh, tender leaves of the nopal and putting them in boxes. My grandmother and my brother Arturo are pulling leaves from the mesquite tree to line the boxes. After we got home my grandfather would shave off all the needles from each leaf of cactus. Then my grandmother would parboil the leaves in hot water. The next morning she would cut them up and stir fry them with chili powder and eggs for breakfast.

Piscando nopalitos

Al comienzo de la primavera, mi abuelo nos venía a buscar y todos íbamos al bosque a piscar nopalitos. Mi abuelo y mi madre están cortando las pencas tiernas del nopal y metiéndolas en cajas. Mi abuela y mi hermano Arturo están recogiendo hojas de mesquite para forrar las cajas. Después que regresábamos a casa, mi abuelo le quitaba las espinas a cada penca del cactus. Luego mi abuela cocía las pencas en agua hirviente. A la mañana siguiente, las cortaba y las freía con chile y huevos para nuestro desayuno.

Hammerhead Shark

This picture is about the times my family went to Padre Island in the Gulf of Mexico to go swimming. Once when we got there, a fisherman had just caught a big hammerhead shark at the end of the pier. How he got the shark to the beach, I never found out. It was scary to see because it was big enough to swallow a little kid whole.

Tiburón martillo

Este cuadro trata de las veces que mi familia iba a nadar a la Isla del Padre en el Golfo de México. Una vez cuando llegamos, un pescador acababa de atrapar a un tiburón martillo al cabo del muelle. Cómo logró llevar al tiburón a la playa, nunca me enteré. Daba mucho miedo ver al tiburón, porque era tan grande que hubiera podido tragarse a un niño pequeño de un solo bocado.

Rabbit

My grandfather used to have a garden and also raise chickens and rabbits. In this painting, he is coming into the kitchen with a freshly prepared rabbit for dinner. My grandmother is making tortillas. That's my little brother, Arturo, sitting on the bench. He liked to watch my grandmother cook. And that's my younger sister, Margie, playing jacks on the floor. I'm watching from my grandparents' bedroom which is next to the kitchen.

Conejo

Mi abuelo tenía un jardín, y también criaba pollos y conejos. En este cuadro, está entrando a la cocina con un conejo que acaba de preparar para la cena. Mi abuelita está preparando tortillas. Ése es mi hermano Arturo, sentado en la banca. Le gustaba mirar a mi abuela mientras cocinaba. Y ésa es mi hermana menor, Margie, jugando a los "jacks" en el suelo. Yo estoy mirando desde la recámara de mis abuelos, que está al lado de la cocina.

LA MEXICANA
S
P

Joseph and Mary Seeking Shelter at the Inn

On each of the nine nights before Christmas we act out the story of Mary and Joseph seeking shelter at the inn. We call this custom "Las Posadas." A little girl and a little boy play Mary and Joseph and they are led by an angel.

Each night the travelers go to a different house. They knock on the door. When the door opens, they sing: "We are Mary and Joseph looking for shelter." At first the family inside refuses to let them in; then the travelers sing again. At last Joseph and Mary are let into the house. Then everybody comes in and we have a party.

Las Posadas

Cada una de las nueve noches antes de Nochebuena, representamos la historia de María y José buscando albergue en la posada. Esta costumbre se llama "Las Posadas". Una niñita y un niñito representan a María y José, y hay un ángel que les guía.

Cada noche, los caminantes van a una casa distinta. Tocan la puerta. Cuando la puerta se abre, cantan: —Somos María y José, buscando posada. Al principio la familia no los deja entrar; entonces los caminantes vuelven a cantar. Por fin dejan entrar a María y José. Luego todos entran y celebran con una fiesta.

Making Tamales

This is a scene from my parents' kitchen. Everybody is making tamales. My grandfather is wearing blue overalls and a blue shirt. I'm right next to him with my sister Margie. We're helping to soak the dried leaves from the corn. My mother is spreading the cornmeal dough on the leaves and my aunt and uncle are spreading meat on the dough. My grandmother is lining up the rolled and folded tamales ready for cooking. In some families just the women make tamales, but in our family everybody helps.

La Tamalada

Ésta es una escena de la cocina de mis padres. Todos están haciendo tamales. Mi abuelo tiene puesto rancheros azules y camisa azul. Yo estoy al lado de él, con mi hermana Margie. Estamos ayudando a remojar las hojas secas del maíz. Mi mamá está esparciendo la masa de maíz sobre las hojas, y mis tíos están esparciendo la carne sobre la masa. Mi abuelita está ordenando los tamales que ya están enrollados, cubiertos y listos para cocer. En algunas familias sólo las mujeres preparan tamales, pero en mi familia todos ayudan.

Rio Grande
CARMEN LOMAS GARZA
©1987

Watermelon

It's a hot summer evening. The whole family's on the front porch. My grandfather had brought us some watermelons that afternoon. We put them in the refrigerator and let them chill down. After supper we went out to the front porch. My father cut the watermelon and gave each one of us a slice.

It was fun to sit out there. The light was so bright on the porch that you couldn't see beyond the edge of the lit area. It was like being in our own little world.

Sandía

Es una noche calurosa de verano. Toda la familia está en el corredor. Mi abuelo nos había traído unas sandías esa tarde. Las pusimos en el refrigerador para enfriarlas. Después de la cena, salimos al corredor. Mi padre cortó la sandía y nos dio un pedazo a cada uno.

Era divertido estar sentados allá afuera. La luz del corredor era tan fuerte que no se podía ver más allá del área que estaba iluminada. Era como estar en nuestro propio pequeño mundo.

Our Lady of San Juan

A mother and son have gone to church and she's doing some praying. In the meantime, her son starts entertaining himself by taking things out of her purse. She lets him for awhile. Then he hands her a handkerchief. I don't know if he thought that maybe she was crying and needed her handkerchief, or whether he was just playing with it and she took it away from him.

Nuestra Señora de San Juan

Una madre y su hijo han ido a la iglesia y ella está rezando. Mientras tanto, el hijo se entretiene sacando cosas de su cartera. Ella se lo permite por un rato. Luego él le entrega un pañuelo. No sé si es que el niño pensó que su madre estaba llorando y necesitaba su pañuelo, o si el niño estaba jugando con el pañuelo y su madre se lo quitó.

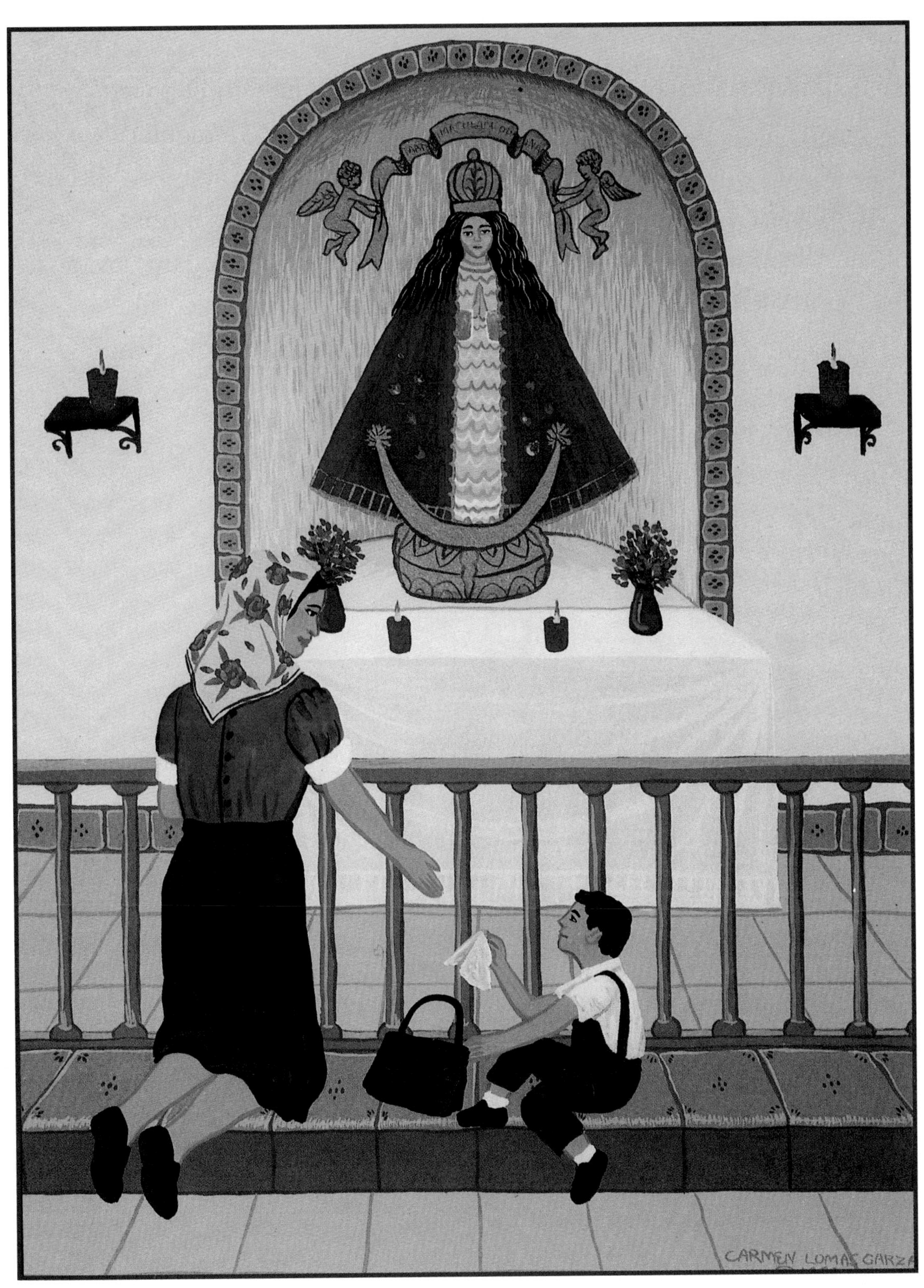
CARMEN LOMAS GARZA

Healer

This is a scene at a neighbor's house. The lady in bed was very sick with the flu. She had already been to a regular doctor and had gotten prescription drugs for her chest cold. But she had also asked a healer, a curandera, to do a final cleansing or healing for this flu. So the curandera came over and did a cleansing using branches from the rue tree. She also burned copal incense in a coffee can at the foot of the bed. Curanderas know a lot about healing. They are very highly respected.

Curandera

Ésta es una escena en la casa de una vecina. La mujer que está en cama estaba muy enferma con influenza. Ya había visto a un doctor y había conseguido una receta médica para sus pulmones. Pero también le había pedido a una curandera que le hiciera una limpieza final o cura para su enfermedad. Así que la curandera vino e hizo una limpieza usando ramas de ruda. También quemó incienso de copal en una lata de café al pie de la cama. Las curanderas saben mucho y ayudan mucho a la gente. Por eso se las respeta tanto.

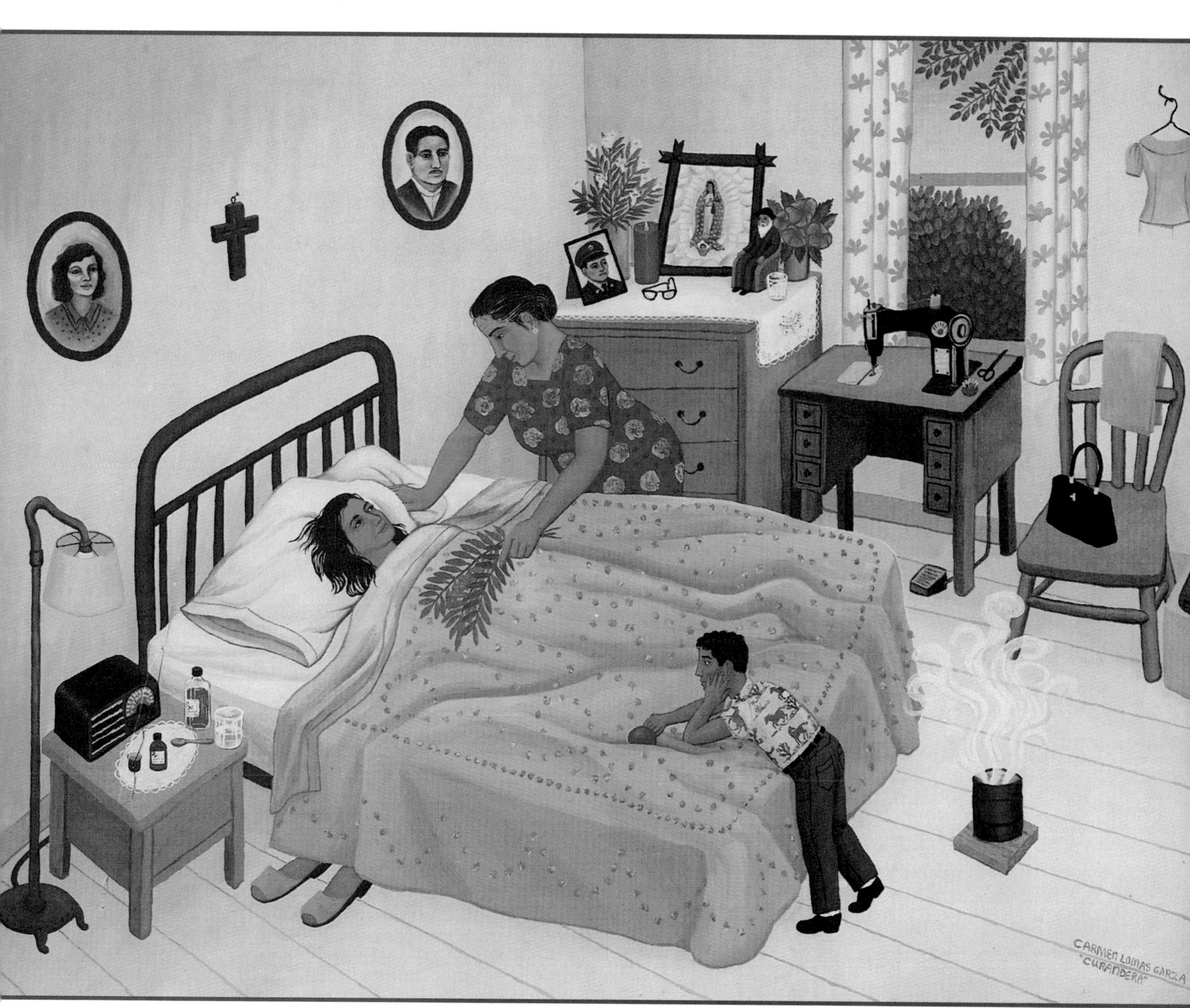
CARMEN LOMAS GARZA
"CURANDERA"

Beds for Dreaming

My sister and I used to go up on the roof on summer nights and just stay there and talk about the stars and the constellations. We also talked about the future. I knew since I was 13 years old that I wanted to be an artist. And all those things that I dreamed of doing as an artist, I'm finally doing now. My mother was the one who inspired me to be an artist. She made up our beds to sleep in and have regular dreams, but she also laid out the bed for our dreams of the future.

Camas para soñar

Mi hermana y yo solíamos subirnos al techo en las noches de verano y nos quedábamos allí platicando sobre las estrellas y las constelaciones. También platicábamos del futuro. Yo sabía desde que tenía trece años que quería ser artista. Y todas las cosas que soñaba hacer como artista, por fin las estoy haciendo ahora. Mi madre fue la que me inspiró a ser artista. Ella nos tendía las camas para que durmiéramos y tuviéramos sueños normales, pero también preparó la cuna para nuestros sueños del futuro.

RESPONDING

All in the Family

Write a Journal Entry

Kingsville, Texas, Here I Come!

If you could visit Carmen Lomas Garza's family, what would you like to do with them? Where would you go? Which foods would you try? Write a journal entry about your visit.

Draw a Picture

Family Album

Do you remember a special day spent with your family? Draw a picture of that day. When you finish, share your picture with your family.

Away from Town

Away from the street lights,
away from town,
stars are more shiny
and hang more down.

Out in the country
where spaces grow,
stars are more many
and hang more low.

Aileen Fisher

City

Langston Hughes

In the morning the city
Spreads its wings
Making a song
In stone that sings.

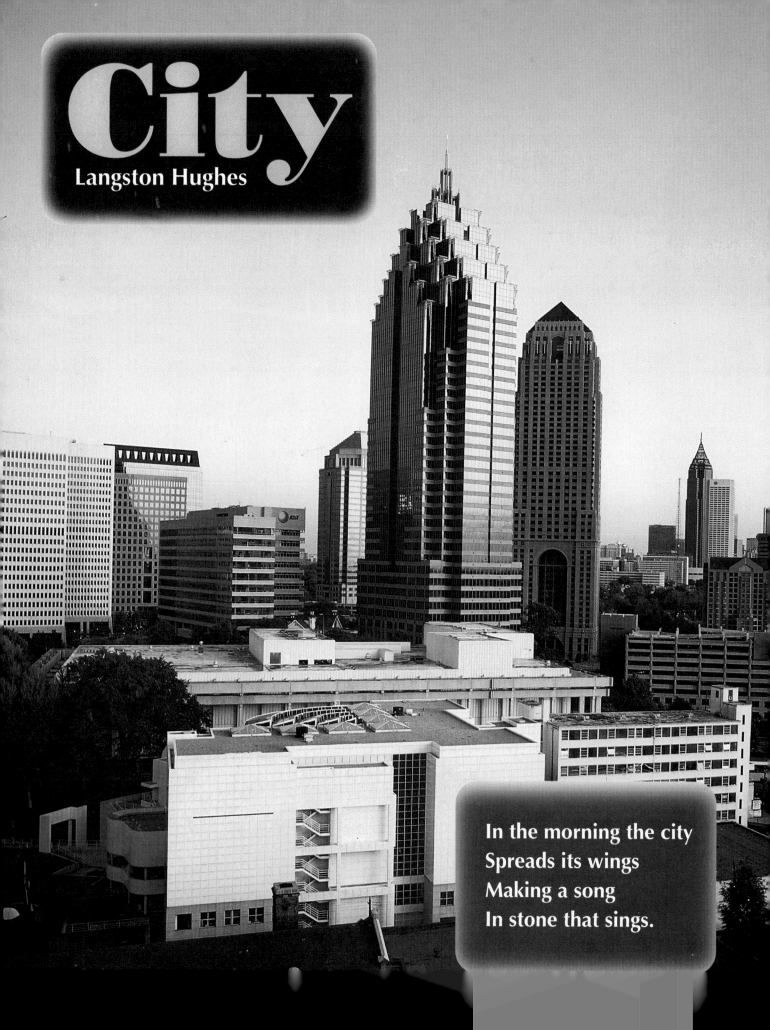

In the evening the city
Goes to bed
Hanging lights
About its head.

from *Earthwise at school*
by Linda Lowery and Marybeth Lorbiecki

What Does Earthwise Mean?

Have you heard about the bad things happening to the earth — oil spills, garbage piles, air pollution, poisoned rivers, and things like that? Don't let them get you down. There are things each one of us can do to make the planet healthier. And we can do them wherever we are — in our apartments or houses, our classrooms or schoolyards, our neighborhood parks or county woods.

First we need to find out as much information as we can about how the earth works. Then we will be able to take actions that make sense for the whole planet — actions that are earthwise.

Cloudy Skies

Since cities are so full of people, factories, and traffic, city air is usually more polluted than country air.

On some days, people in large cities, such as Los Angeles and Mexico City, are told to stay indoors as much as possible. The air outside is too dirty to breathe.

What is your city or town like? Count the smokestacks near you. Ask the factory owners what chemicals they put into the air and what they are doing to stop polluting.

Stand on a street corner, and count the cars that go by. How many people does each car carry? Could these people get around town in a different way? Ask people in your neighborhood what they think can be done. Are they doing anything? Are you?

Air Test

How can you test the air you breathe every day?

Spread a thin layer of petroleum jelly on the inside of two wide-mouth glass jars.

Place one jar on a shelf in your classroom. Place the other jar in a safe location outside.

After one week, compare the jars. Which jar is darker? What do you think caused this? If either of the jars shows a lot of pollution, what are you going to do? It's probably time to do more research. Call your national, state, or city pollution-control agency and ask them to do an official test of the air near and in your school.

Fewer Cars = Cleaner Air

Even if we could clean up all the smoke from factories, the air would still not be clean. Why not?

Because the exhaust from cars, trucks, and planes is one of the greatest causes of air pollution. So what can you do about that? Plenty!

Walk, skateboard, bike, in-line skate, or roller-skate to places. Share car rides. Take buses, subways, and trains.

Make it a game with your friends and family to see how little you can use a car. Keep track of your miles. Try to go one or two miles less by car each week.

City Solutions

- If every two or more persons in the U.S. going to school or work rode together, we would save more than 600,000 gallons of gasoline every day. Think of how much less air pollution there would be!
- In Boulder, Colorado, there are Bike-to-Work days. Prizes are awarded to the companies with the most employees riding bikes to work.

Tree Treasures

One of the chemicals put into the air when coal, oil, wood, or gasoline is burned is carbon dioxide. Some carbon dioxide is good for the earth. But too much carbon dioxide traps the sun's heat close to the earth. Then our climate becomes too hot.

This overwarming is called the greenhouse effect. Fortunately, there is a way to clean the air and fight the greenhouse effect — plant trees. Trees absorb carbon dioxide, and they make shade. Every tree you plant makes the earth cleaner and cooler.

How to Plant a Tree

1. Get permission from the owner of the land.
2. Keep the roots moist and handle them gently.
3. Pick a spot that gets some sun each day.
4. Dig a hole twice as big as the roots.
5. Hold the tree in the hole, and gently cover the roots with dirt. Pack the dirt down gently to remove any air pockets.
6. Water thoroughly right away and then once every day for the first week. Afterward water once a week, if you can.

Meet the Author

Belinda Rochelle grew up hearing stories about the great boxer Joe Louis from her grandparents. They used to listen to his fights on the radio, back in the days when few people owned televisions and boxing wasn't televised. *When Jo Louis Won the Title* is a story about those days.

Meet the Illustrator

Larry Johnson knew he wanted to be an artist ever since he was in the third grade. In addition to illustrating sports books such as *The Jesse Owens Story*, Johnson works as a sports cartoonist for the *Boston Globe* and has his own publishing company.

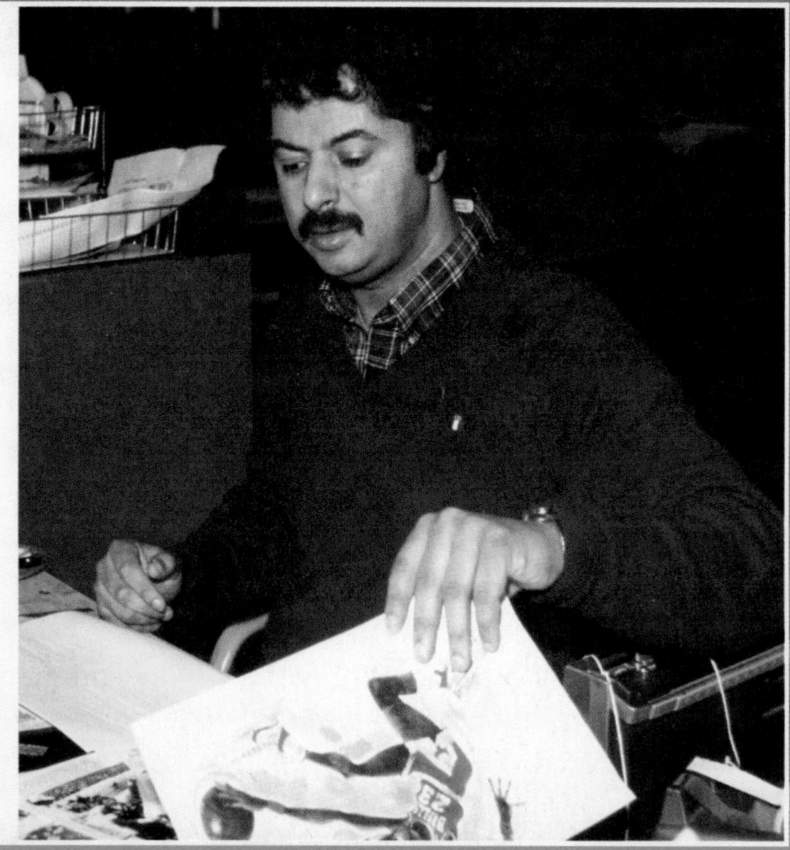

When Jo Louis Won the Title

Belinda Rochelle Illustrated by Larry Johnson

JO LOUIS sat perched on the top step of ten steps, waiting for her grandfather, John Henry.

"Is that my favorite girl in the whole wide world?" he said as he strolled up the street. He leaned over and picked up Jo Louis, swung her round and round until her ponytails whirled like the propellers of a plane, swung her round and round until they were both dizzy with gasps, swung her round and round until they were both dizzy with giggles.

John Henry's brown eyes twinkled as he returned Jo Louis to the top step and sat down next to her. The smile quickly disappeared from Jo Louis's face. "Why such a sad face on a pretty girl?" he asked.

Tomorrow was a special day for Jo Louis. The first day at a new school. "I don't want to go to school!" Jo Louis said to her grandfather. "I don't want to be the new girl in a new neighborhood at a new school."

John Henry put his arm around her and pulled her close. "Why don't you want to go to school?" he asked.

"I'll probably be the shortest kid in class, or I'll be the one who can't run as fast as the other kids. I finish every race last."

"It's just a matter of time before a new school is an old school. Just a matter of time before you'll be able to run really fast, and you won't always finish last," he said, patting her hand. "What's the real reason you don't want to go to school?" John Henry asked.

Jo Louis shook her head. It was hard to explain. She just knew it would happen. Someone would ask THE question. IT was THE question, the same question each and every time she met someone new: *"What's your name?"*

It was that moment, that question, that made Jo Louis want to disappear. And it really wouldn't make a difference if she were taller, and it wouldn't make a difference that she was the new kid in school, and it wouldn't make a difference if she could run really fast. She just wished that she didn't have to tell anyone her name.

Her grandfather picked her up and placed her on his knee. "Let me tell you a story," he said.

"When I was just a young boy living in Mississippi," he began, "I used to dream about moving north. To me it was the promised land. I wanted to find a good job in the big city. Cities like Chicago, St. Louis.

"But everybody, I mean everybody, talked about Harlem in New York City. Going north, it was all anybody ever talked about. I would sit on the front porch and just daydream about those big-city places. The way some folks told it everything was perfect. Even the streets in the big city were paved with gold, and it was all there just waiting for me."

John Henry's eyes sparkled as his voice quickened. "When I saved enough money, I crowded onto the train with other small-town folks headed north. Everything I owned fit into a torn, tattered suitcase and a brown box wrapped in string.

"I rode the train all day and all night. Like a snake winding its way across the Mississippi River, that train moved slowly through farmlands and flatland, over mountains and valleys, until it reached its final destination."

Jo Louis closed her eyes. She loved her grandfather's stories — his words were like wings and other things. She listened closely until she felt she was right there with him.

"'New York City! New York! New York!' the conductor bellowed as the train pulled into the station.

"I headed straight to Harlem. I had never seen buildings so tall. They almost seemed to touch the sky. Even the moon looked different in the big city. The moonlight was bright and shining, the stars skipped across the sky. The streets sparkled in the night sky's light. It was true! The streets did seem to be paved in gold!

"I walked up and down city streets that stretched wide and long. I walked past a fancy nightclub, where you could hear the moaning of a saxophone and a woman singing so sad, so soft, and so slow that the music made me long for home.

"And then, all of a sudden the sad music changed to happy music. That saxophone and singing started to swing. Hundreds of people spilled out into the sidewalks, waving flags, scarves, waving handkerchiefs and tablecloths. Hundreds of people filled the streets with noise and laughter, waving hats and anything and everything, filling the sky with bright colors of red, white, green, yellow, blue, purple, and orange.

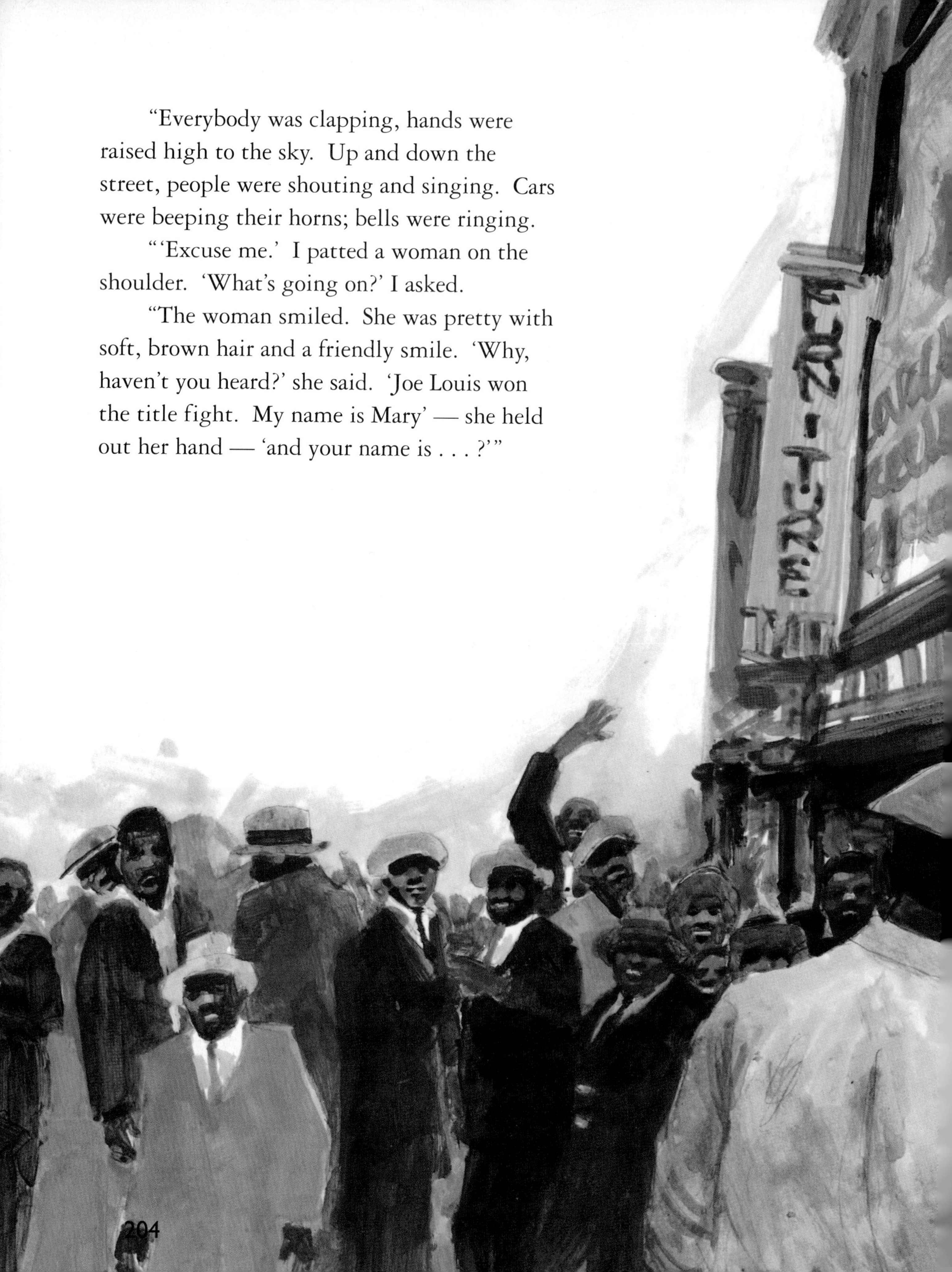

"Everybody was clapping, hands were raised high to the sky. Up and down the street, people were shouting and singing. Cars were beeping their horns; bells were ringing.

"'Excuse me.' I patted a woman on the shoulder. 'What's going on?' I asked.

"The woman smiled. She was pretty with soft, brown hair and a friendly smile. 'Why, haven't you heard?' she said. 'Joe Louis won the title fight. My name is Mary' — she held out her hand — 'and your name is . . . ?'"

FURNITURE
PRICES

John Henry smiled and hugged Jo Louis close. "It was a special night for me. It was a special night for black people everywhere. Joe Louis was the greatest boxer in the world. He was a hero.

"That night he won the fight of his life. A fight that a lot of people thought he would lose. Some folks said he was too slow, others said he wasn't strong enough. But he worked hard and won. It was a special night, my first night in the big city, and Joe Louis won the fight. But the night was special for another reason."

"It was the night you met Grandma," Jo Louis said, and she started to smile.

"It was a special night that I'll never forget. I named your father Joe Louis, and he named you, his first child, Jo Louis, too." Her grandfather tickled her nose. "That was the night you won the title. You should be very proud of your name. Every name has a special story."

The next day Jo Louis took a deep breath as she walked into her new school classroom and slipped into a seat.

The boy sitting next to Jo Louis tapped her on the shoulder. "My name is Lester. What's your name?"

Jo answered slowly, "My name is Jo . . . Jo Louis." She balled her fist and closed her eyes and braced herself. She waited, waited for the laughter, waited for the jokes. She peeked out of one eye, then she peeked out the other eye.

"Wow, what a great name!" he said, and smiled.

Name Your Choice

Make a Mural

Let's Celebrate!

Jo Louis's grandfather told her about a celebration that he remembered. Think about a special event that happened in your community. Who was there? What did you do? With your classmates, make a mural showing the event.

Share a Personal Story

A Great Name

There's an interesting story about how Jo Louis got her name. Is there a story behind *your* name? Maybe you were named after a relative, or perhaps you have a nickname. Tell your classmates the story. If you don't know a story about your name, make one up.

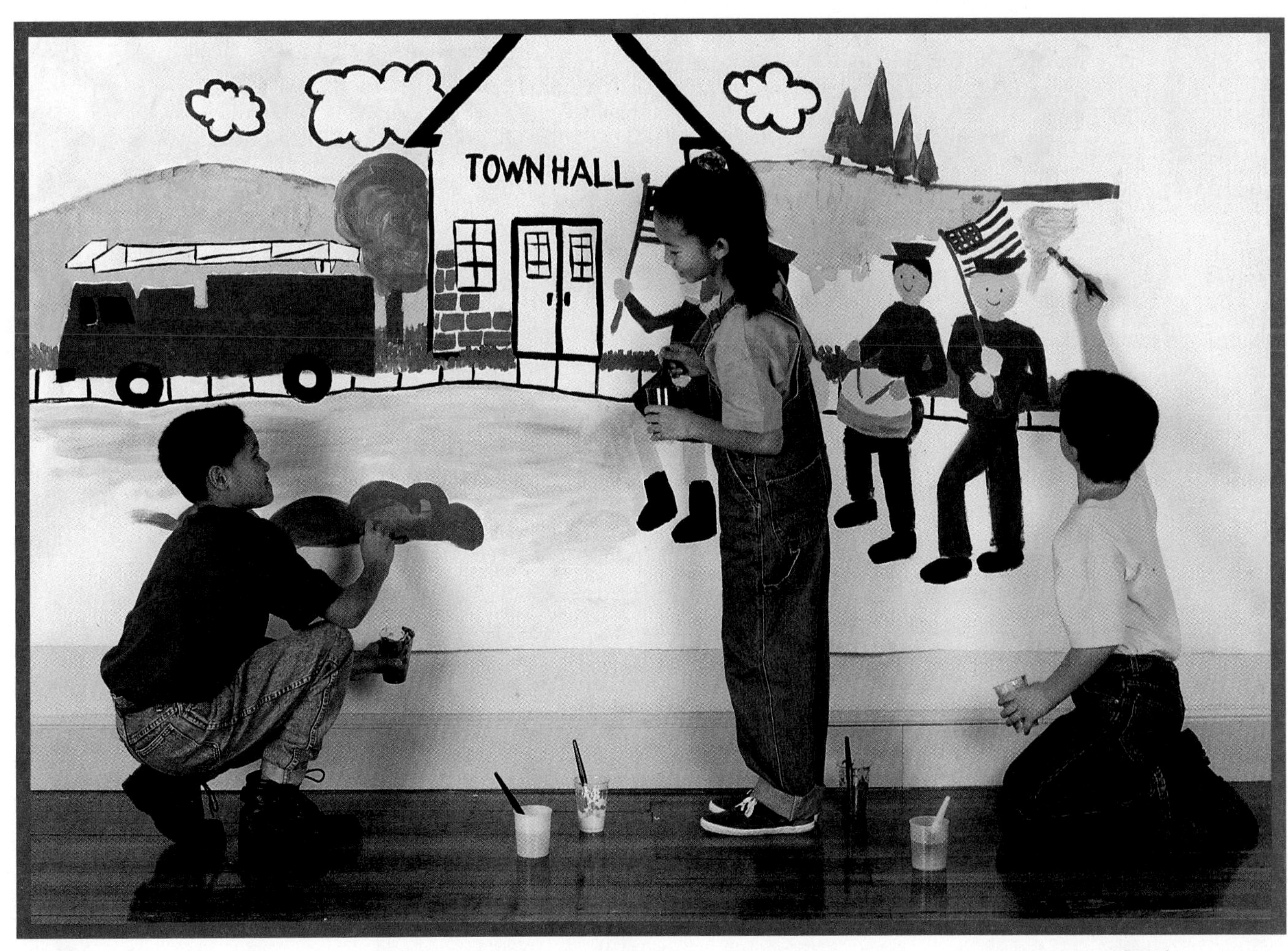

BE A WRITER

The Pool Somersault

A True Story by Joyce Hsieh

When something happened to Joyce at her neighbor's pool, she decided to write about it.

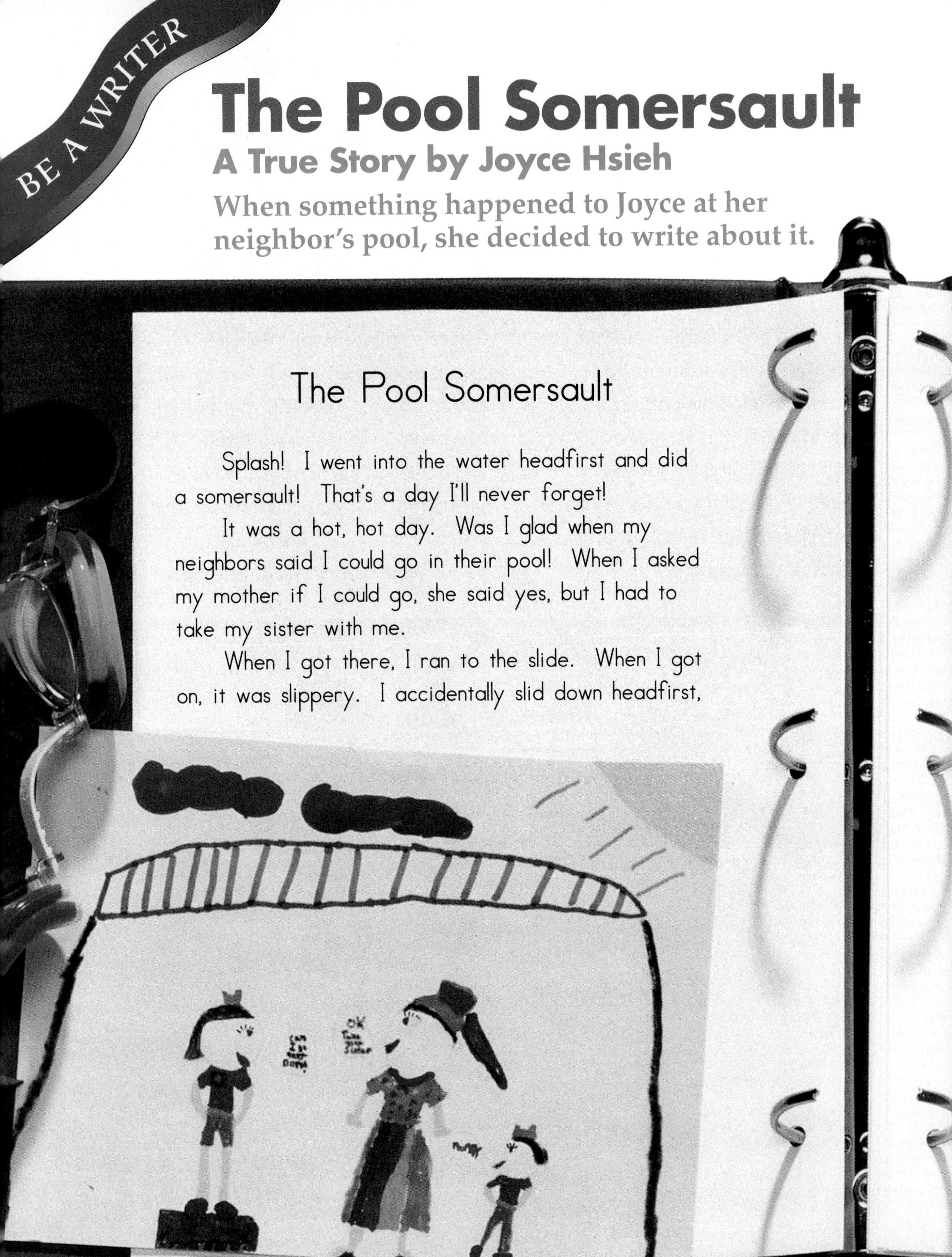

The Pool Somersault

Splash! I went into the water headfirst and did a somersault! That's a day I'll never forget!

It was a hot, hot day. Was I glad when my neighbors said I could go in their pool! When I asked my mother if I could go, she said yes, but I had to take my sister with me.

When I got there, I ran to the slide. When I got on, it was slippery. I accidentally slid down headfirst, and the rest of my body went into the water in a somersault! I could not believe it! It was the first time that I ever did a somersault in the water. When I went into the water, it was exciting and scary all at the same time. It gave me a good feeling after it was over because I'd never done a somersault in the water before, but I landed so badly. My leg was bleeding and even had a little hole in it. It hurt, but I didn't cry or anything. My neighbor's baby, Chuckie, and my sister were staring at me, and they laughed at me. Both tried to copy me, but I stopped them. I was worried that they would fall down and break something.

When I got home, I told my mom what happened. She seemed surprised but glad that I didn't hurt myself too badly. What an exciting day that was!

Joyce Hsieh

Paloma Elementary School
San Marcos, California

Joyce likes to write about animals, places she has been, and her family. She also likes to write letters to friends. She chose to write about the pool somersault because it was fun and interesting. Playing games, tennis, and the piano are some things that Joyce enjoys doing. When she grows up, Joyce wants to be an artist.

Painting the Town

oil paint

turpentine

linseed oil

Coming to the Celebration
Mattie Lou O'Kelley, 20th century
oil paint

palette knife

oil brushes

The Builders
Jacob Lawrence, 1974
silk screen print

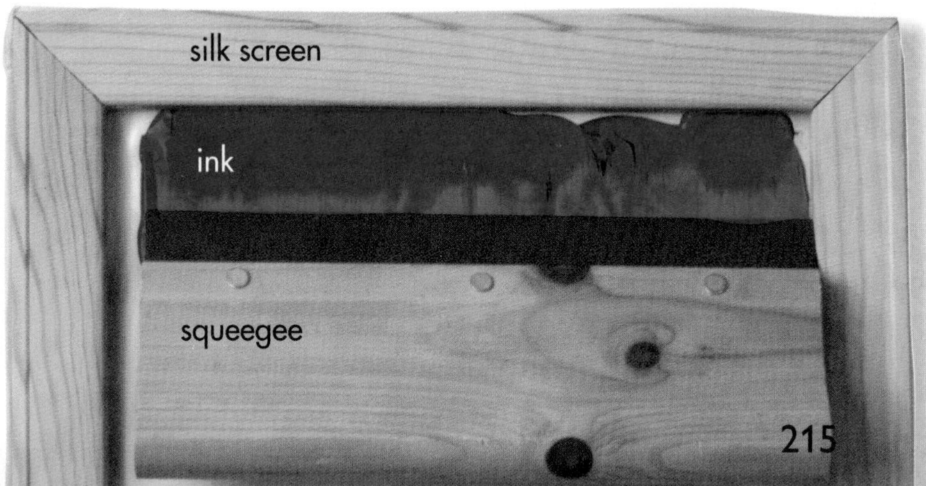

Shawnee Indians Having Cornbread Dance

Earnest Spybuck, c. 1910
watercolor

sketch
pencil

watercolor
paper

watercolor
paint

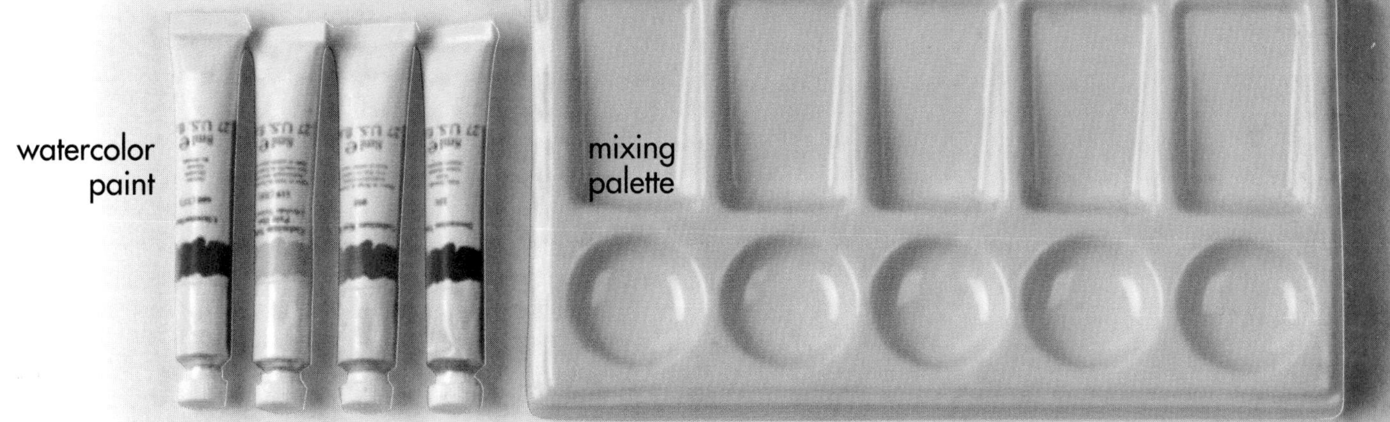

May Day, Central Park

Maurice Prendergast, 1901
watercolor

DISASTER!

DISASTER!

Contents

DISASTER! Read On Your Own

The BRAVEST DOG EVER
The True Story of Balto
By Natalie Standiford
Illustrated by Donald Cook

PAPERBACK **PLUS**

The Bravest Dog Ever: The True Story of Balto

by Natalie Standiford

A dog-sled team races against time to save a town from a deadly illness.

In the same book . . .

Photos and information about Balto, an article about dog-sled racing, and more.

Anna, Grandpa, and the Big Storm

by Carla Stevens

A ride on the elevated train in the Great Blizzard of 1888 turns into an adventure for a young girl and her grandfather.

In the same book . . .

More about the time and place, and information about blizzards.

More Tales of Survival

If You Lived at the Time of the Great San Francisco Earthquake

by Ellen Levine

It's 1906, and you are there for one of the biggest earthquakes in history.

Oil Spill!

by Melvin Berger

In 1989, 11 million gallons of oil spilled into waters off the Alaskan coast. What did it take to clean it up?

Clouds of Terror

by Catherine A. Welch

It's a peaceful day on the farm — until the sky is filled with swarms of hungry grasshoppers.

They Survived Mount St. Helens

by Megan Stine

Day becomes dark as night when a volcano erupts in Washington State.

Meet the Author

When **Judy Donnelly** was eight years old, she read *Treasure Island* and immediately began searching for treasure in her neighborhood. She never found any, but that didn't stop her from loving a good treasure hunt. Today, Donnelly writes stories about true-life treasure hunts, such as *Tut's Mummy Lost — and Found.*

Meet the Illustrator

John Gamache enjoys bringing history to life. Before beginning each illustration for *The Titanic: Lost . . . and Found*, he would first imagine himself in each scene. He said, "I began to understand how scary it must have been to leave the ship in those tiny lifeboats in the middle of the night."

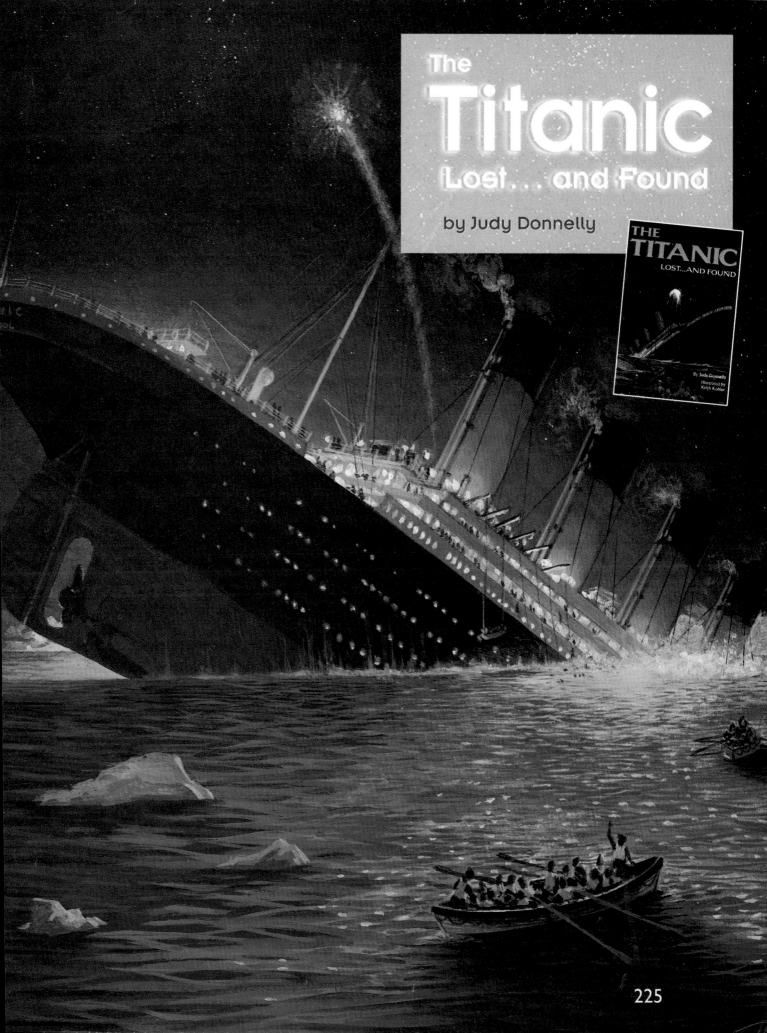

The Titanic Lost . . . and Found

by Judy Donnelly

THE TITANIC LOST...AND FOUND

By Judy Donnelly

Illustrated by Keith Kohler

TITANIC

1

THE WONDER SHIP

It is April 10, 1912.

The whole world is talking about an amazing new ship. Its name is the *Titanic*.

The ship is getting ready to leave on its first trip across the ocean. It is going all the way from England to America.

Newspapers call the *Titanic* "The Wonder Ship." They say it is like a floating palace. The *Titanic* has restaurants, a post office — even a gym with a toy camel to ride.

Edward J. Smith, captain of the *Titanic*

This picture shows the ship as if it were sliced open. The fancy rooms are on the top decks. On the lower decks you can see the squash court and the swimming pool.

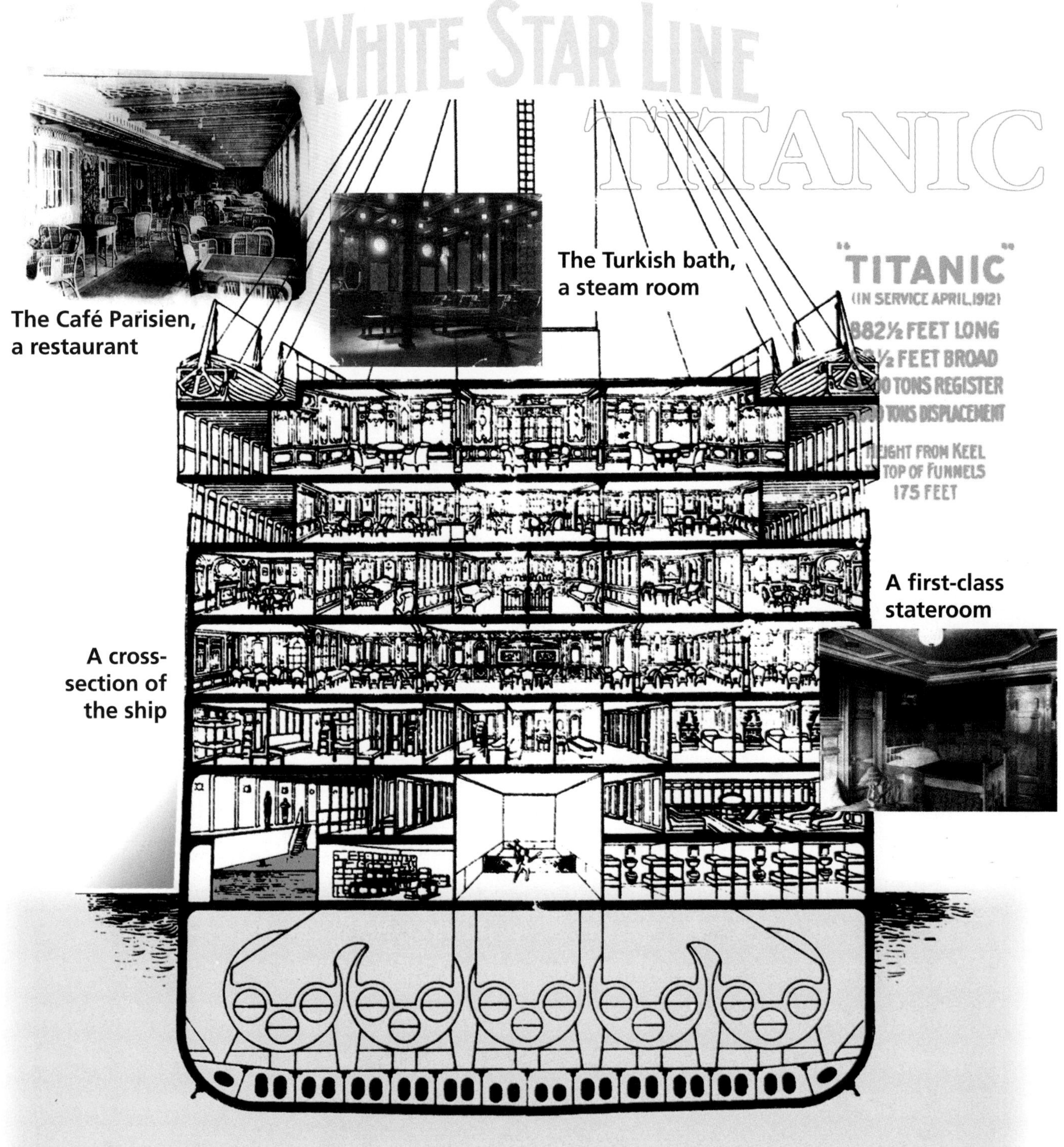

The *Titanic* is the biggest ship the world has ever seen. The ship is almost four city blocks long and is as tall as an eleven-story building.

Best of all, experts say the *Titanic* is the safest ship ever. They say it cannot sink. Why? The ship doesn't have one bottom — it has two. One is inside the other.

The lowest part of the *Titanic* is divided into sixteen watertight compartments. If one compartment starts to flood, the captain can just pull a switch. A thick steel door will shut. The water will be trapped. It cannot flood the rest of the ship. Two or three or even four compartments can be full of water. Still, the *Titanic* will float.

TITANIC

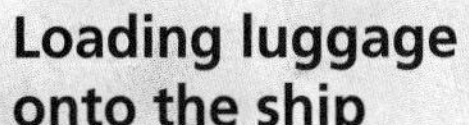

Loading luggage onto the ship

The *Titanic* has another nickname — "The Rich Man's Special." Some of the richest people in the world are sailing on the *Titanic*. Their tickets cost more money than a sailor earns in a lifetime.

Not all the passengers are rich. Some have very little money. They are not traveling for fun. They are going off to find a new home in America.

At last the big moment comes. The *Titanic* is ready to sail!

Crowds line the shore. Passengers come out on the decks. They wave good-bye to their friends.

The *Titanic* has begun its first voyage. No one guesses this will also be its last.

2

ICEBERG

It is April 14, 1912. The *Titanic* is in icy waters off the coast of Canada.

It is almost midnight. The ship is quiet. The sea is smooth as glass. The air is biting cold.

The passengers have had a good dinner. Some of them are still up playing cards. Most are asleep in their rooms.

It is a good night to be inside. But the lookout must watch for danger. He is high above the ship in the crow's-nest. He stares into the darkness.

Suddenly the lookout sees a dark shape. It is a mountain of ice! And the *Titanic* is heading right into it! The lookout rings an alarm. He calls, "Iceberg straight ahead!"

Captain Smith

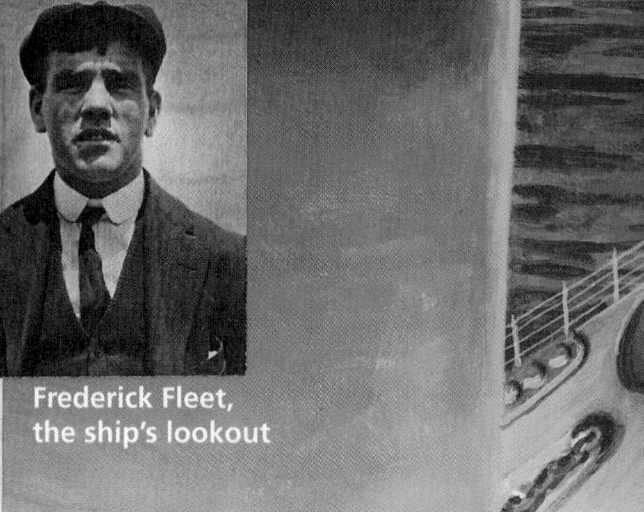

Frederick Fleet, the ship's lookout

A seaman is below, steering the ship. He tries to turn the ship away. But it is too late.

The giant iceberg scrapes along the side of the ship.

There is a bump. A grinding noise. It doesn't seem like much. Some people do not even notice.

But the captain hurries from his room. He goes down below. He wants to see if the ship is hurt. Soon he learns the terrible truth.

The iceberg has hurt the ship badly. Water is pouring in. Five of the watertight compartments are already flooded. And that is too many. Nothing can be done now.

It seems impossible. But it is true. The *Titanic* is going to sink!

The captain gives his orders. Wake the passengers! Radio for help! And make the lifeboats ready!

The captain is afraid. He knows that 2,227 people are on board. And there are only enough lifeboats for 1,178 of them.

The passengers do not know this. As people come out on deck, they laugh and joke. Some are in evening gowns. Others wear life jackets over pajamas. But they are not worried. They still think they are on a ship that cannot sink.

Get in the lifeboats, the sailors tell them. Women and children go first. Men go only if there is room.

Many do not want to get in. The big ship seems so safe. The little lifeboats do not.

The sailors are in a hurry. They know there is trouble. They rush people into the lifeboats. Some are only half full, but the sailors lower them anyway.

Many passengers are far from the lifeboats. They are the poor ones. Their rooms are down below. They know there is trouble too. But they do not know where to go. A few try to find their way. They go up stairs and down halls. Some are helped by seamen. Most just wait below.

In the radio room the operator calls for help. Other ships answer. But they are many, many miles away.

One ship is not far away. Its name is the *Californian*. This ship is fewer than twenty miles from the *Titanic*. It could reach the sinking ship in minutes and save everyone.

The *Titanic*'s operator calls again and again. But the *Californian* does not answer. It is late at night and the ship's radio is turned off. No one on board hears the calls for help.

The *Titanic* tries to signal the *Californian*. It sets off rockets that look like fireworks. Sailors on the *Californian* see the rockets. But they do not understand that the *Titanic* is in trouble. And so they do not come.

On the *Titanic* the band is playing. The music is cheerful. But people are afraid now. The deck is slanting under their feet.

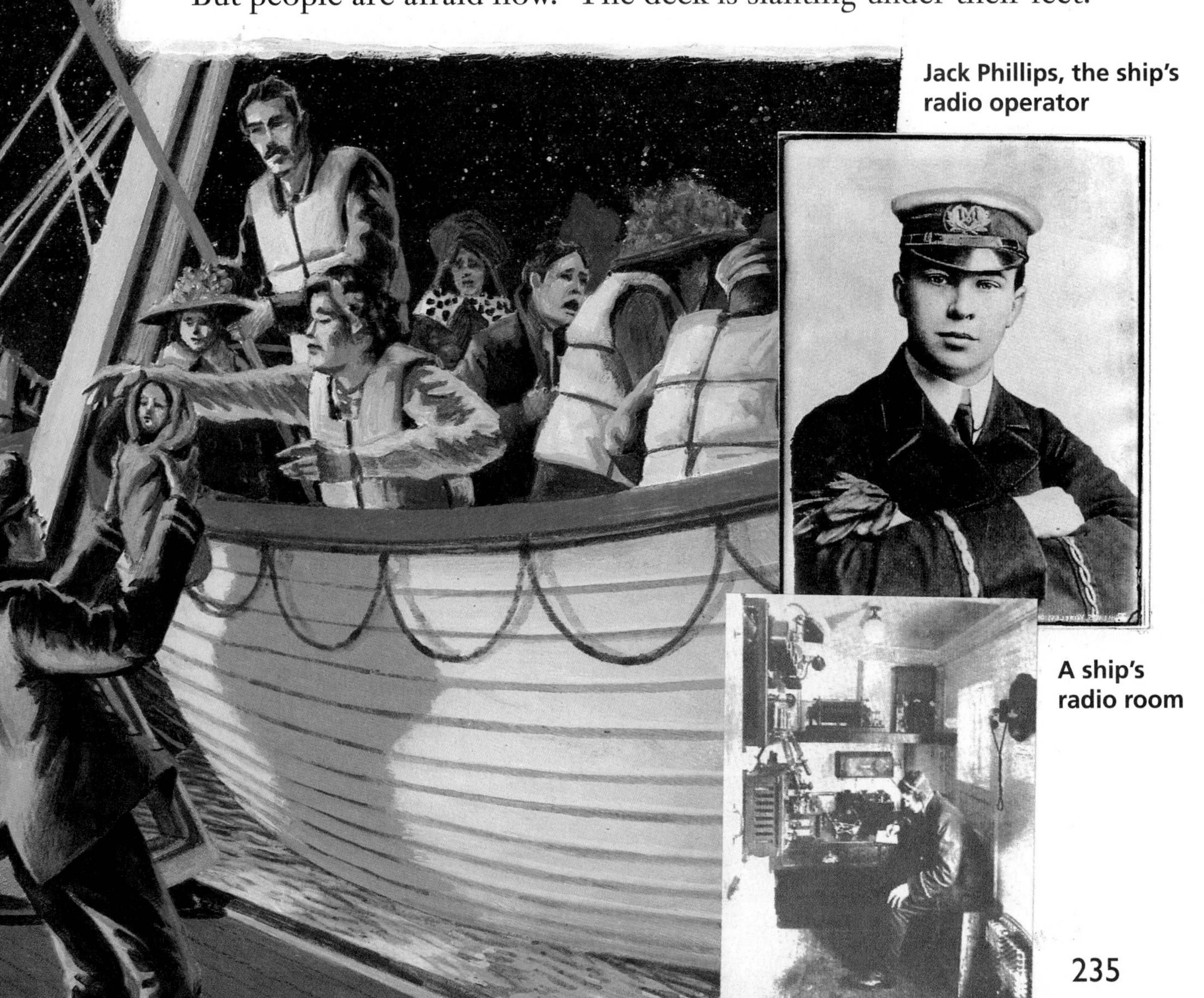

Jack Phillips, the ship's radio operator

A ship's radio room

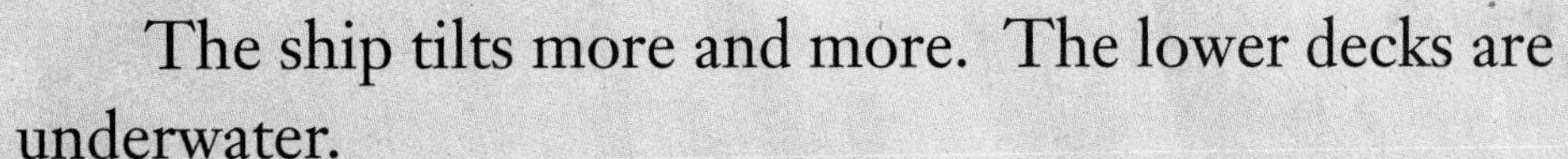

The ship tilts more and more. The lower decks are underwater.

Two lifeboats are left, but the sailors cannot get them loose. Hundreds and hundreds of people are still on board. And by now they know the end is near.

An old couple holds hands. The wife will not leave her husband. One man puts on his best clothes. "I will die like a gentleman," he says.

Some people jump into the icy water. A few are lucky. They reach a lifeboat.

Benjamin Guggenheim (right) and Isidor and Ida Straus (far right), passengers who lost their lives

A pocket watch found on a passenger who died

The people in the lifeboats row away from the *Titanic*. Everyone is staring at the beautiful ship. Its lights are sparkling. The lively music drifts across the water.

Then the music changes. The band plays a hymn.

One end of the huge ship slides slowly into the ocean. The music stops. There is a great roaring noise. A million sparks fill the air. The other end of the ship swings straight up.

For a moment the *Titanic* stays pointed at the stars. Then it disappears under the black water.

Members of the ship's band

3

NEVER AGAIN

It is 2:20 A.M. on April 15. The *Titanic* is gone.

The people in the lifeboats stare into the night. The sky is full of shooting stars. But it is dark. And it is bitter, bitter cold.

Most of the lifeboats have drifted away from each other.

People just wait. And they try to get warm. Some have fur coats. Others are wearing bathrobes and slippers. One man is in nothing but his underwear. Coldest of all are the ones who jumped from the ship and swam to a boat. Their hair and clothes are frosted with ice.

One lifeboat is upside down. About thirty men are standing on it. They lean this way and that to keep the boat from sinking. Icy waves splash against their legs.

One lifeboat goes back to try and help. They save one man. He is floating on a wooden door. They do not find many others. No one can last long in the freezing water.

Hours pass. The sky grows lighter. It seems as if help will never come. Then suddenly a light flashes. And another. It is a ship — the *Carpathia*. It has come from fifty-eight miles away.

Everyone waves and cheers. They make torches. They burn paper, handkerchiefs — anything. They want to make the ship see them.

The sun begins to rise. There are icebergs all around. The rescue ship almost hits

Survivors on board the *Carpathia*

one, but it turns just in time. The ship keeps heading toward the lifeboats.

Help has finally come.

All eyes are on the rescue ship. Boat by boat, the people are taken aboard. The sea is rough and it takes many hours. But at last everyone is safe.

A lifeboat being picked up by the *Carpathia*

The rescue ship *Carpathia*

Survivors of the disaster

THE WEATHER.
The New York Times.
"All the News That's Fit to Print."
NEW YORK, TUESDAY, APRIL 16, 1912.—TWENTY-FOUR PAGES.
ONE CENT
TITANIC SINKS FOUR HOURS AFTER HITTING ICEBERG;
866 RESCUED BY CARPATHIA, PROBABLY 1250
ISMAY SAFE, MRS. ASTOR MAYBE, NOTED NAM
Col. Astor and Bride, Isidor Straus and Wife, and Maj. Butt Aboard.
"RULE OF SEA" FOLLOWED
Women and Children Put Over in Lifeboats and Are Supposed to be Safe on Carpathia.
PICKED UP AFTER 8 HOURS
Vincent Astor Calls at White Star Office for News of His Father and Leaves Weeping.
FRANKLIN HOPEFUL ALL DAY
Manager of the Line Insisted Titanic Was Unsinkable Even After She Had Gone Down.
HEAD OF THE LINE ABOARD
J. Bruce Ismay Making First Trip on Gigantic Ship That Was to Surpass All Others.
The Lost Titanic Being Towed Out of Belfast Ha
CAPT. E. J. SMITH,
TITANIC
DISASTER
GREAT LOSS
OF LIFE
EVENING NEWS

Soon the news flashes all around the world. The unsinkable *Titanic* has sunk. More than 2,200 people set out. Only 705 are rescued. How? Why? No one can understand.

When the rescue ship reaches New York, thousands of people are waiting. The *Titanic* survivors tell their stories. The world learns the truth. The safest ship was not safe at all.

It was too late for the *Titanic*. But it was not too late for other ships.

New safety laws were passed. Many changes were made. Today every ship must have enough lifeboats for every single passenger. And every ship has lifeboat drills so people know what to do if there is an accident.

Ship radios can never be turned off. Every call for help is heard.

And now there is a special ice patrol. Patrol airplanes keep track of dangerous icebergs. They warn ships. Never again can an iceberg take a ship by surprise.

The *Titanic* was a terrible loss. But the world learned from it.

Crowds awaiting news in New York City

J. J. Astor died; his wife, Madeleine, survived.

4

FOUND AT LAST

Years went by. The *Titanic* lay more than two miles down in black, icy cold water.

No divers could go down in such deep water. And no one could even find the ship. The map below shows you roughly where the *Titanic* sank.

Some people thought the *Titanic* had been crushed. They said it was probably in a million pieces.

Yet treasure hunters kept on dreaming of the wonderful ship. They were sure there was gold on board — and diamonds and pearls.

A man named Robert Ballard dreamed of the *Titanic* too. Robert was a scientist. He studied the oceans.

Robert worked in a famous laboratory in Woods Hole, Massachusetts. He didn't care about treasure. He just wanted to find the ship. He thought about it for years.

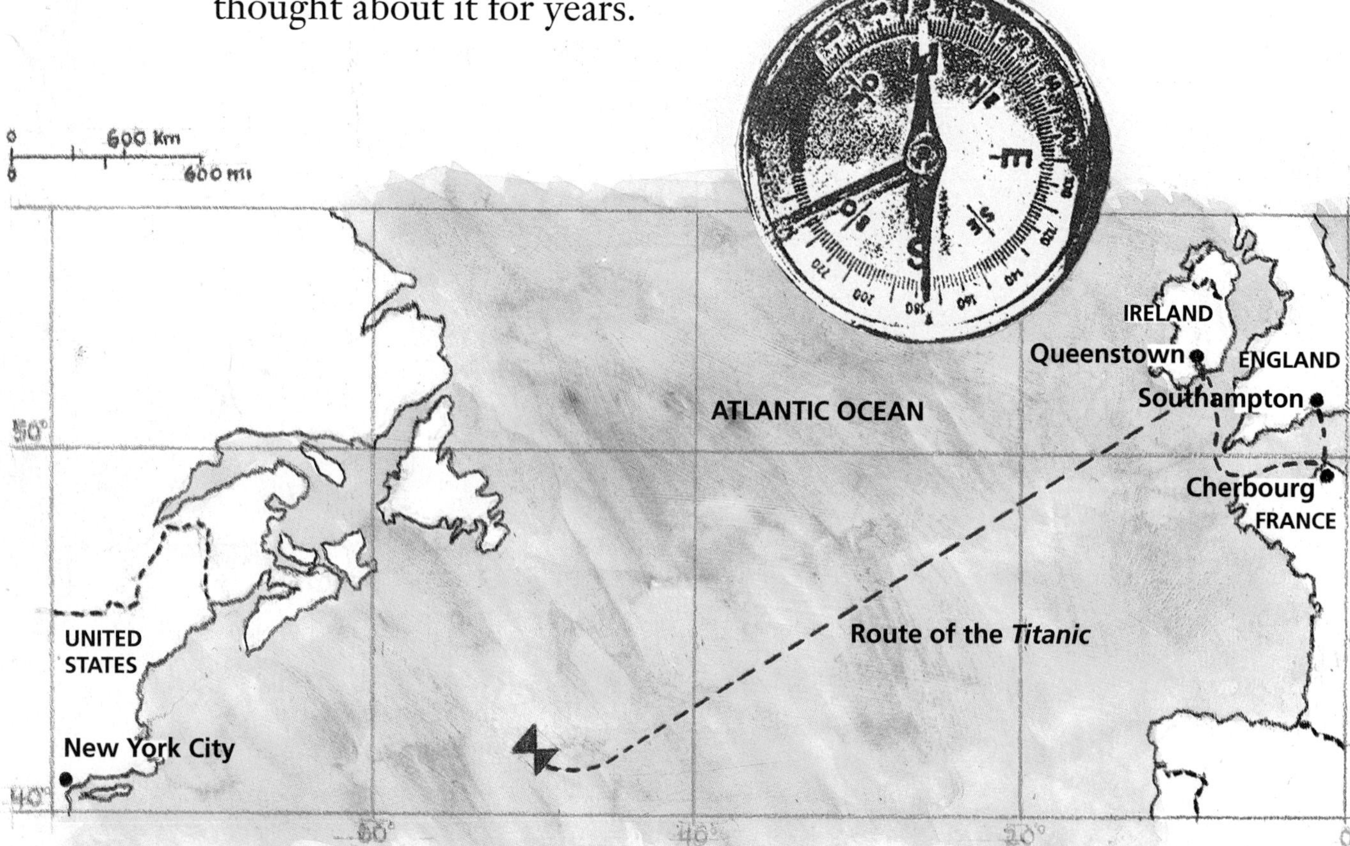

Robert had a special invention. It was a kind of underwater robot. Its name was *Argo*.

Argo could dive down very, very deep. It had lights and a video camera. It could skim along the ocean floor. It could take underwater video pictures. And it could send them to TV screens on a ship.

Robert read all about the *Titanic*. He looked at maps and photos. Finally he was ready. He thought he knew where the mystery ship was waiting.

In the summer of 1985, Robert sailed to the island of St. Pierre, south of Newfoundland. He went with a team of scientists. He took *Argo* with them.

Robert sent *Argo* hunting. He didn't even have to get his feet wet. But he had to do a lot of watching. For days it was the same. He saw sand and more sand.

Robert Ballard

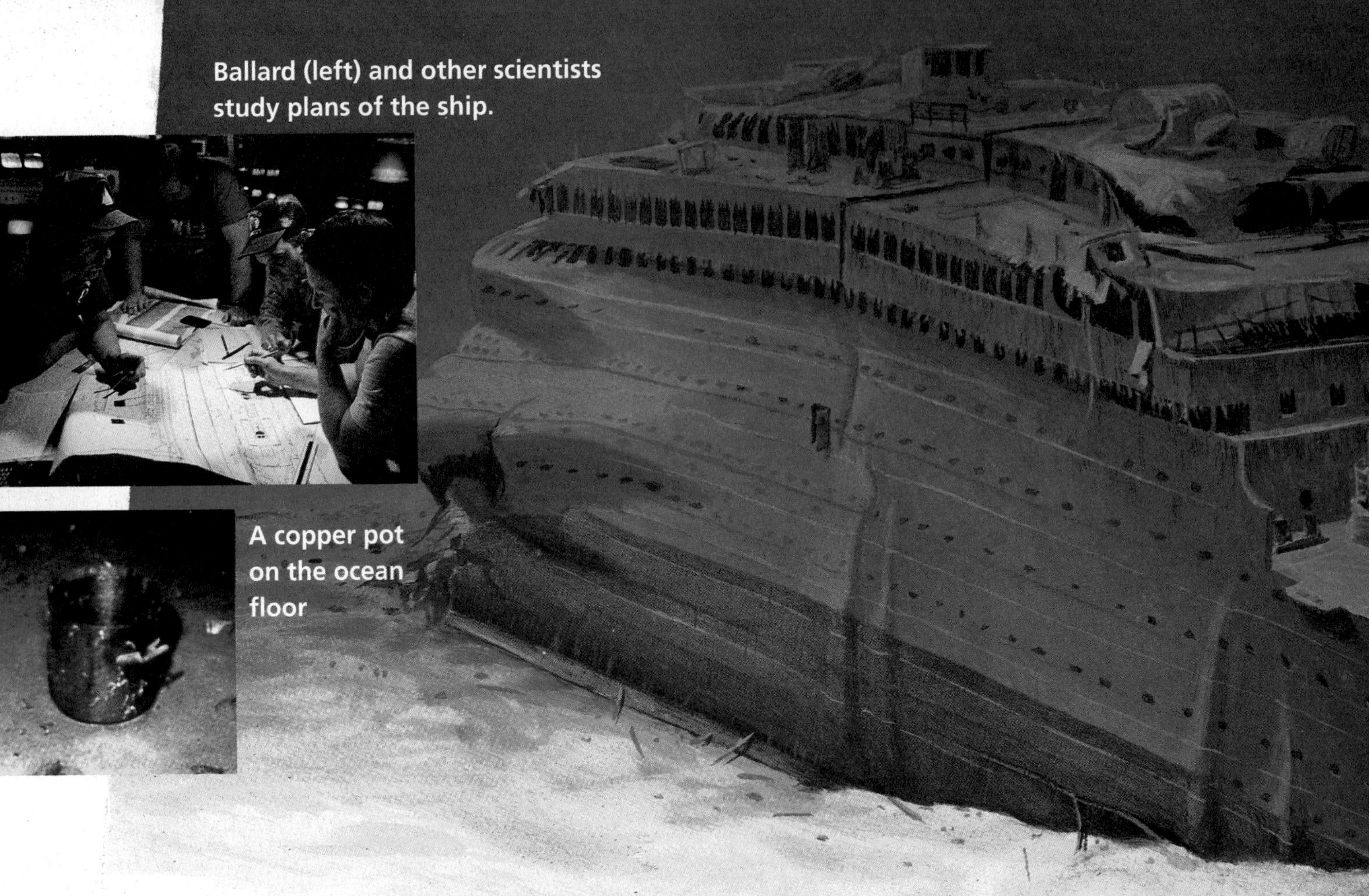

Ballard (left) and other scientists study plans of the ship.

A copper pot on the ocean floor

Then at last something different flashed on the screen. Was it a ship? Yes, it was. A huge ship.

The other scientists began to cheer. They had done it. They had found the *Titanic*!

Robert could not believe his eyes. It was like seeing a ghost. There was the *Titanic*, sitting on the ocean floor. It had broken apart. But Robert could see how beautiful it still was.

Over the days Robert saw more and more of the ship. He saw the crow's-nest where the lookout first spotted the iceberg. A beautiful glass window lay in the sand. The ship's giant anchors were there. Bottles of wine were scattered about. And suitcases.

It was amazing. And it was sad. So many people had set out on the voyage. So few had returned.

Finally Robert sailed home. He did not tell anyone where he found the *Titanic*. He hoped the ship would stay just as it was. He did not want treasure hunters to come and loot it.

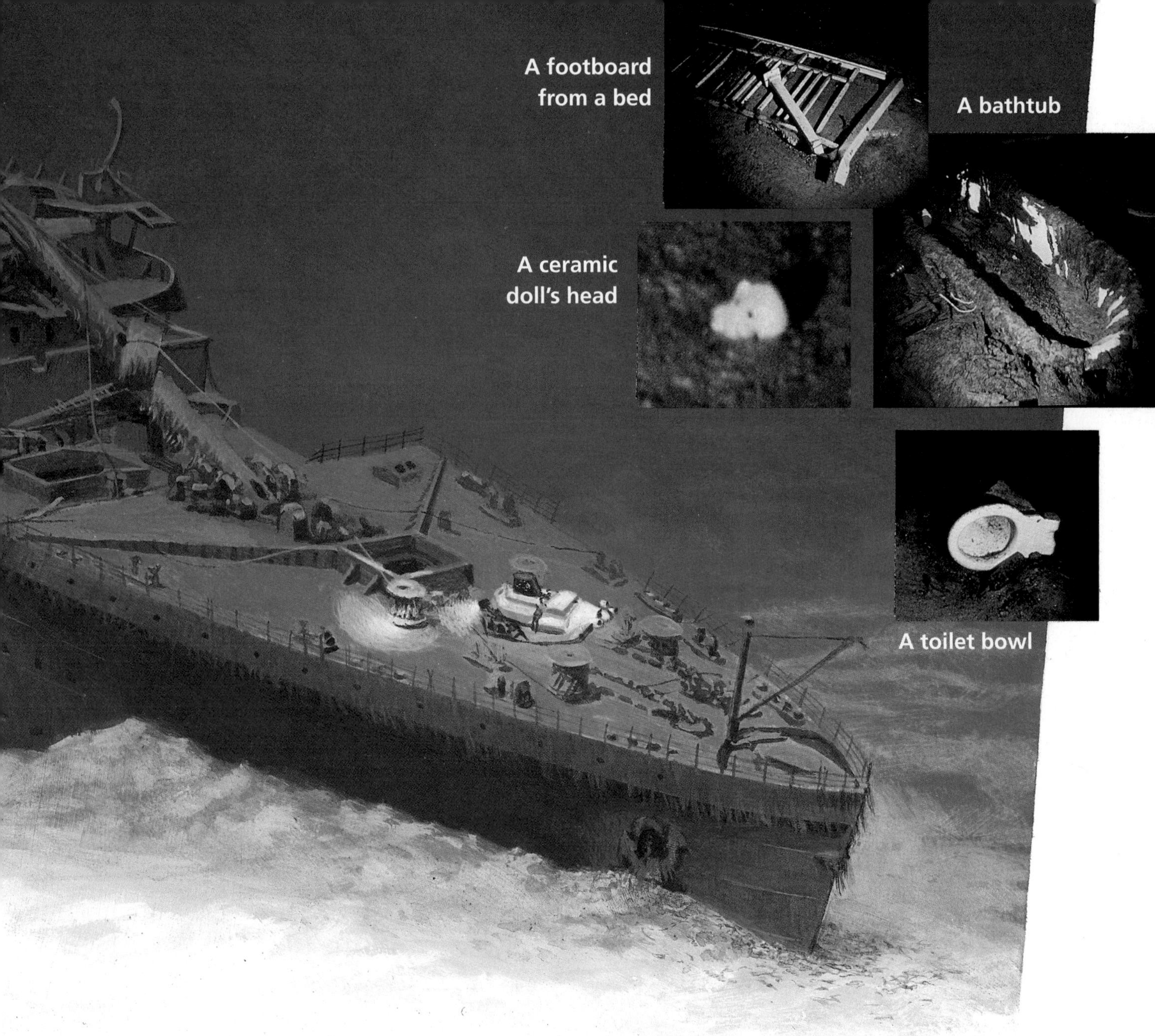

Robert wanted to go back to the *Titanic*. And a year later he did. He landed a small submarine right on the deck of the *Titanic*. He sent a robot inside the ship.

Robert did not take anything. But he did leave something behind. It was a message. He left it for anyone else who might find the *Titanic*. It asked that the great ship be left in peace.

All over the world people were thrilled by Robert's work. To some, it was very special. They had sailed on the *Titanic*.

They had been small children then. Now they were very old. But they had never forgotten the "unsinkable *Titanic*."

The world would never forget.

RESPONDING

Staying on Course

Write an Article

Extra! Extra!

Write a newspaper article about the *Titanic.* You can be either a reporter from the year 1912, when the great ship sank, or a reporter from the year 1985, when the wreck was discovered.

Play a Quiz Game

Did You Know . . . ?

Write questions and answers about the disaster on index cards. Then quiz your friends. Here's one to get you started: "Who was the captain of the *Titanic*?"

Titanic Trivia

by A.F.J. Marshello

1. How much did it cost to build *Titanic*?
2. How many rivets were used in the construction of *Titanic*?
3. How many people made up the crew of *Titanic*?
4. How many women were among *Titanic's* crew?
5. Who was President of the United States in 1912?
6. Who was on the British throne when *Titanic* sailed?
7. How much did John Jacob Astor pay for his stateroom in 1912?
8. How much did it cost to travel Third Class on *Titanic*?
9. How many meals were served each day aboard *Titanic*?
10. How many teaspoons were aboard?
11. How much tea was carried aboard *Titanic*?
12. How many eggs were aboard *Titanic*?
13. How much fresh meat was aboard?
14. How many heads of lettuce were aboard?

Answers:

How much did it cost to build *Titanic*?

Approximately 8 million dollars

How many rivets were used in the construction of *Titanic*?

3,000,000

How many people made up the crew of *Titanic*?

Approximately 900

How many women were among *Titanic's* crew?

23

Who was President of the United States in 1912?

William Howard Taft

6

Who was on the British throne when *Titanic* sailed?

King George V

How much did John Jacob Astor pay for his stateroom in 1912?

$3,300

How much did it cost to travel Third Class on *Titanic*?

Approximately $30

How many meals were served each day aboard *Titanic*?

Approximately 6,000

How many teaspoons were aboard?

Approximately 6,000

How much tea was carried aboard *Titanic*?

Approximately 1,000 pounds

How many eggs were aboard *Titanic*?

Approximately 35,000

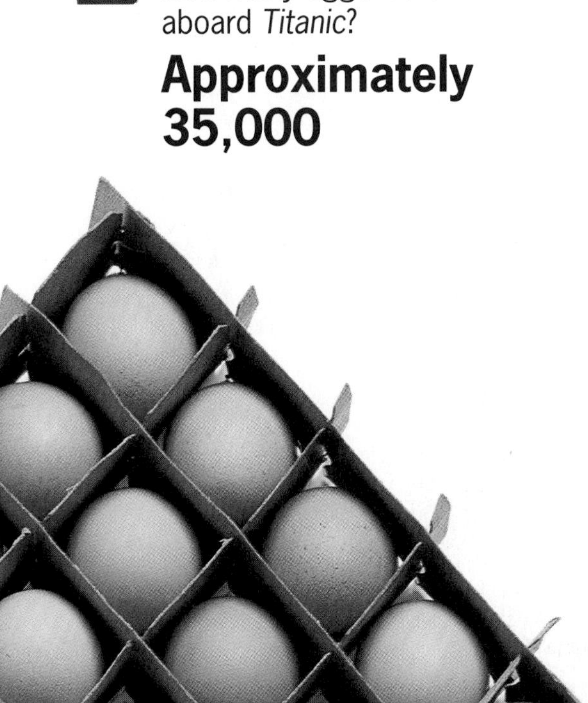

13 How much fresh meat was aboard?

Approximately 75,000 pounds

How many heads of lettuce were aboard?

Approximately 7,000

THE TITANIC

a folk song

Lively 𝅗𝅥 = 108

1. O they built the ship Ti - ta - nic to sail the o - cean blue, And they thought they had a ship that the water would never leak through, But the Lord Al - migh - ty's hand knew this ship would ne - ver stand, It was sad when that great ship went down.

CHORUS

It was sad, it was sad, It was sad when that great ship went down, Hus - bands and wives, lit - tle chil - dren lost their lives, It was sad when that great ship went down.

1. O they built the ship *Titanic* to sail the ocean blue,
And they thought they had a ship that the water would never leak through,
But the Lord Almighty's hand knew this ship would never stand,

It was sad when that great ship went down.
It was sad, it was sad,
It was sad when that great ship went down,
Husbands and wives, little children lost their lives,
It was sad when that great ship went down.

2. O they sailed from England and were almost to the shore,
When the rich refused to associate with the poor,
So they put them down below, where they were the first to go,
(Chorus)

3. The *Titanic* left the harbour at a rapid speed,
She was carrying everything that the people need,
She sailed six hundred miles away, met an iceberg on her way,
(Chorus)

4. It was on a Monday morning just about four o'clock,
When the ship *Titanic* felt that terrible shock,
People began to scream and cry, sayin' "Lord, am I going to die?"
(Chorus)

5. The boat was full of water, the sides about to burst,
When the captain shouted, "A-women and children first."
O the captain tried to wire, but the lines were all on fire,
(Chorus)

6. Now the ship began to settle and they all tried to flee,
And the band it struck up, "Nearer My God to Thee,"
And Death came ridin' by, sixteen hundred had to die,
(Chorus)

About the Author

Edith Kunhardt

Edith Kunhardt calls herself a "hands-on researcher," meaning she likes to experience the things she writes about. For a book about firefighters, for example, she rode around with a fire chief. A book about Pompeii led her to the ancient city in Italy, where she is pictured at left.

About the Illustrator

Robert G. Steele

Illustrating is often a family project for Robert Steele. His wife and children help out by putting on costumes and posing for his historical drawings. For ideas, Steele looks through his collection of photos and sketches, covering hundreds of subjects "from Ancient Rome to Zebras."

POMPEII . . . Buried Alive!

by Edith Kunhardt

1

The Sleeping Giant

Once there was a town named Pompeii (pom-PAY). Near the town there was a mountain named Vesuvius (veh-SOO-vee-us).

The people in Pompeii liked living by the mountain. It was a good place to grow grapes. It was a good place to raise sheep. And — it looked so peaceful!

But the mountain was really a dangerous volcano. It was like a sleeping giant. If the giant woke up, it could destroy the town. Did the people know about the danger? No, they did not!

A volcano is a special kind of mountain. It has a hole at the top.

One day — almost two thousand years ago — something was happening under Vesuvius. Way down deep it was very, very hot. It was so hot that rock was melting. As the rock melted, a gas was made. The gas was trying to escape.

The gas and the melted rock were mixed together. The mixture was hot and bubbly. The gas was pushing the melted rock up through Vesuvius. The melted rock was about to blast right out the hole at the top!

The day started out the way it always did. The sun rose. People began coming to Pompeii with things to sell. Fishermen were bringing fish. Peddlers were bringing melons and straw hats. Farmers were bringing vegetables. Shepherds were bringing sheep. Carts rumbled through the narrow gates and into town.

The noisy carts in the streets woke up the people in the houses. The family who lived in one of the biggest houses was soon busy.

The mother went to pray in the courtyard. She put flowers by the statue of a god. The father began to dress. His slave helped him. The children were playing. They were glad it was summer. The slaves in the kitchen were making breakfast.

No one in the house knew that something terrible was going to happen.

After breakfast the children went outside. The streets were crowded. People were at work inside the shops.

Bakers were busy baking flat bread. Weavers were busy weaving wool cloth. Potters were busy making clay pots. Slaves were getting water at a fountain. A musician was playing his flute.

No one in the street knew that something terrible was going to happen.

By late morning many men were at the bathhouse. They were having a good time. Some men were playing ball. Some men were lifting weights. Some men were talking in the steam room. Others were soaking in the hot pools. The father from the big house was there. His slave was rubbing oil on his back.

No one at the bathhouse knew that something terrible was going to happen.

By noon the town meeting place was full of people. Some people were looking for things to buy. Some people were talking to their friends. Lawmakers were meeting to make new laws. Visitors were looking at the beautiful buildings. The mother from the big house was there. She was praying in the temple.

No one in the town meeting place knew that something terrible was going to happen.

2

The Giant Wakes Up

Suddenly the ground began to tremble. All of the houses in Pompeii began to shake. The giant was waking up!

Then there was an enormous cracking sound. The top of Vesuvius blew off! A huge cloud of dust and ash came pouring out!

Everyone began to scream. People came out of their houses to look at the huge cloud. Shopkeepers came out of their shops. Bakers forgot about their bread. Farmers forgot about their fruits and vegetables. And lawmakers forgot about the new laws.

The cloud was getting bigger and bigger. The cloud hid the sun. It was dark. Tiny hot pebbles began to fall on the people in Pompeii.

Some people found pillows to cover their heads. Others hid inside their houses. Everyone was running and pushing and shoving and shouting. Some people ran toward the town gates to get away. Others went home to protect their jewelry and gold coins. A few went to the temple to pray. Could the gods save them?

The day became as dark as night. A horrible smell filled the air. It was like rotten eggs.

People rushed toward the sea. A few held torches to light the way. The sea was wild. Huge waves kept crashing onto the beach. Fish were left flopping in the sand.

The family from the big house was able to get into a boat. They were able to get away.

When the pebbles fell on Pompeii, many people could not escape. They were trapped under the pebbles.

Then hot ashes began pouring out of the volcano. The ashes fell on the people. The ashes were hot enough to make hair sizzle!

The people in the streets tried to protect themselves. They hid in corners and behind walls. They covered their faces with their hands and clothes.

But the ashes piled up higher and higher. The people could not move. The people could not breathe. They were trapped under the ashes. The ashes kept falling!

Heaps of ashes filled the streets. The ashes spilled into the houses. They piled up to the first-story windows. They piled up to the second-story windows. The people inside the houses were trapped too.

But Vesuvius was not done! Now a great cloud of poisonous gas rushed out of the mountain. The cloud covered Pompeii.

A great river of hot ashes and gases raced down the side of the mountain. The river flowed right over the walls of the town. No one in Pompeii was saved.

Across the bay a boy stood watching. His name was Pliny (PLIN-ee). Pliny saw the strange cloud that came out of Vesuvius. He saw the darkness over Pompeii. Later he heard about the hot ashes and pebbles and the wild sea. Did Pliny ever forget that day? No, he did not!

3
Buried Alive!

The ashes fell on Pompeii for two days. Then it was over. The huge cloud was gone. The mountain was quiet.

The ashes cooled and became hard. Only the tops of buildings showed above them. The whole town had been buried alive!

Some of the people who had left in boats came back. They came to look for their houses. They came to look for their belongings. They came to look for their friends. But everything was sealed under the ashes.

Pliny grew up. He became a writer. He wrote about the huge cloud that came out of Vesuvius. He wrote about the volcano that buried Pompeii.

Many years went by. Vesuvius erupted again and again. More ashes fell on the town. At last there was no sign that anyone had ever lived there. By and by, people forgot about the town named Pompeii.

Hundreds of years later the ashes on top changed into soil. Grass began to grow. People built houses right above the buried town. They built a new town on top of Pompeii. They did not even know that the old town was there!

Then people began to read Pliny's letters. They read about a buried town named Pompeii. Where was Pompeii? Nobody knew.

One day some workers were digging a tunnel for water. They found pieces of an old wall under the ground. But they did not know that the wall was part of a town.

Many years later more people came to dig in the same place. They found more buildings. Was there a town under the ground? Was it the town Pliny wrote about?

Then one of the diggers found a stone. It had a name carved on it. The name was POMPEII.

People were very excited. The lost town of Pompeii was right there — under their feet! If they could uncover it, they could see how people lived long ago.

Scientists began digging. They worked slowly and carefully. They used many tools. They brushed away the ashes. They did not want to destroy anything.

The scientists found beautiful gold bracelets. They found unbroken eggs. They found pictures made of colored stones. These pictures are called mosaics (mo-ZAY-iks).

And they found the people who had died. At first the scientists found only a few skeletons. Then they saw strange holes in the hard ashes. They poured plaster into the holes. When the plaster dried, the plaster casts were shaped just like people!

The plaster casts showed how the people looked when they died. There was even a plaster cast of a dog on a chain.

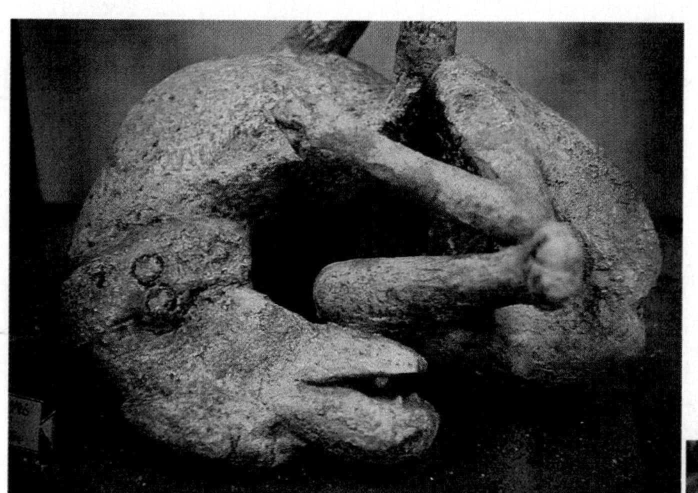

Today the old town of Pompeii is like a great big museum without a roof. Pompeii is in Italy. People come from many lands to visit. They want to see the shops and houses of long ago.

And they want to see Vesuvius, too. It is the most famous volcano in the world.

Scientists watch the volcano very carefully. How much gas is coming out of the ground? How hot are the rocks near the volcano? How much does the earth shake?

Look! A farmer is taking care of his grapevines. They grow on the side of the mountain named Vesuvius. Nearby a lizard is resting on a warm rock.

It is a peaceful day in Pompeii. The giant is sleeping. When will the giant wake up again? Nobody knows.

Have a Blast!

RESPONDING

Build a Diorama

Create a Mini Pompeii

Work with a partner to create a diorama of Pompeii. The diorama might show Pompeii before or during the eruption or as it is today. Display your diorama in the classroom.

Make a Brochure

Have a Nice Trip

If you went to Pompeii today, what would you do and see there? Write a travel brochure to make people want to visit Pompeii. Include maps and illustrations.

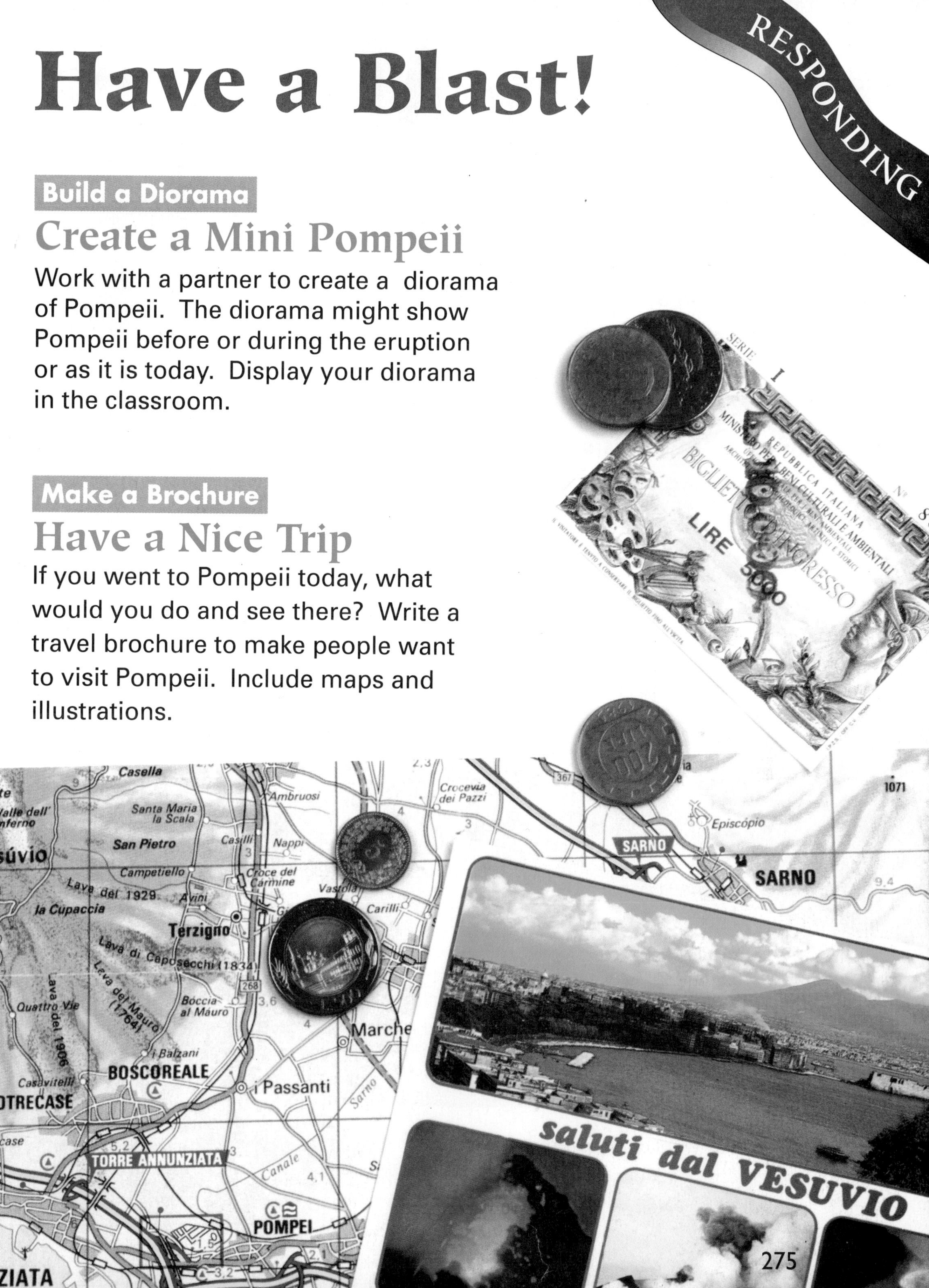

History Makers

The power of volcanic eruptions is hard to imagine, but let's try. Imagine living in Australia and hearing a volcano erupting 2400 miles (3800 km) away in Indonesia. Imagine looking through your camera and seeing the summit of Mount St. Helens disappear. Imagine piloting a jetliner and having volcanic dust stall all four of your engines. Volcanoes are among the most awesome forces in nature. Discover for yourself some of the world's most famous volcanoes.

▲ Kilauea has been erupting since 1983. Lava pours into the ocean where it cools and hardens into rock. As long as Kilauea erupts, the island of Hawaii keeps growing.

In A.D. 79, the eruption of Mount Vesuvius buried the Roman city of Pompeii and left a time capsule of Roman life to be discovered centuries later. Under a 20-foot (6-meter) layer of hardened ash, archaeologists found houses and bodies. A bakery still had bread in the oven. ▼

▲ **M**ount Pinatubo in the Philippines erupted in June 1991. The ash from the volcano was so thick that people had to drive with their car headlights on during the day. Gas clouds from the volcano lowered temperatures around the world.

◀ **T**he 1883 eruption of Krakatau in Indonesia was one of the largest natural explosions in history. It sent rock and ash into the sea, which produced huge sea waves called *tsunamis* (tsoo-NAM-mee).

Some volcanoes can be dangerous even if they are not erupting. In 1986, a cloud of carbon dioxide killed 1700 people, and cows and other animals in Cameroon in Africa. Nearby Lake Nyos, which fills a volcanic crater, was the source of the gas. Over hundreds of years, carbon dioxide seeped up from the volcano into Lake Nyos. No one knows what happened to release the gas into the air. ▼

▲ Although it wasn't large, the 1985 eruption of Nevado del Ruiz in Colombia was hot enough to trigger a mudflow. Melting snow and ice killed 20,000 people.

Mount St. Helens

Before its eruption on May 18, 1980, Mount St. Helens was a perfectly shaped stratovolcano, built by many eruptions over 40,000 years. The 1980 eruption tore 1300 feet (400 m) off the mountain's top and left the crater shaped like a horseshoe.

A prisoner on the island of Martinique in the Caribbean was one of two survivors of the 1902 eruption of Mount Pelée. The thick walls of his jail cell protected Auguste Ciparis from the eruption that killed 28,000 other people. Rescued after four days, and badly burned, Ciparis later joined the Barnum and Bailey Circus. ▶

The volcano's heat melted snow and ice. Thick, smelly mud raced down the North Toutle River Valley below the volcano. The mud swept through houses and carried off cars.

Forests were leveled by rock blasted from the mountain at speeds of up to 200 miles (320 km) per hour. Despite the destruction, plants started growing on the mountainside again in a few months.

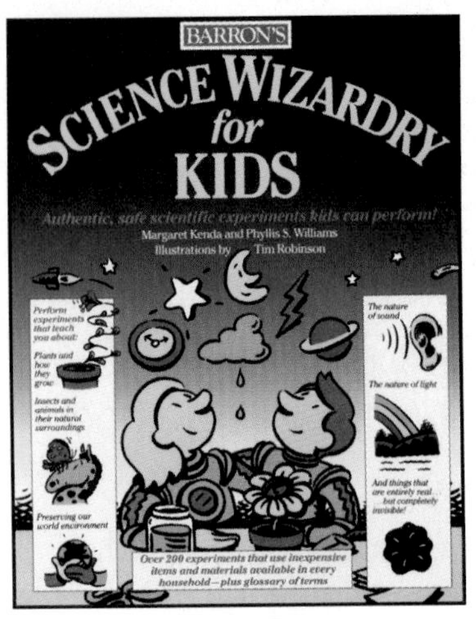

by Margaret Kenda
and Phyllis S. Williams

Construct your own small volcano, and make it erupt.

Here's what you need:

- A shallow box or pan
- Three colors of modeling clay in natural-looking colors such as green, brown, dark gray, black, or red
- A container such as the small cover from a spray can, if you wish
- 1/4 cup (60 ml) water
- 1 tablespoon (15 ml) baking soda
- A few drops of red food coloring
- A few drops of liquid dishwashing detergent
- 1/4 cup (60 ml) vinegar

1 Use the shallow box or pan to hold your volcano.

2 Use the modeling clay to model your volcano. Make the body of the volcano a natural-looking color. Next, use dark red or dark brown modeling clay to create the lava flowing down the sides of the volcano.

3 Scoop out a hole at the very tip of the volcano. If you wish, put in a container.

4 Pour the water into the hole or into the container at the tip of the volcano. Stir in the baking soda, red food coloring, and liquid dishwashing detergent.

5 Just as you're ready for your volcano to erupt, pour in the vinegar. The base (baking soda) and the acid (vinegar) combine to produce a good bubbling-over effect.

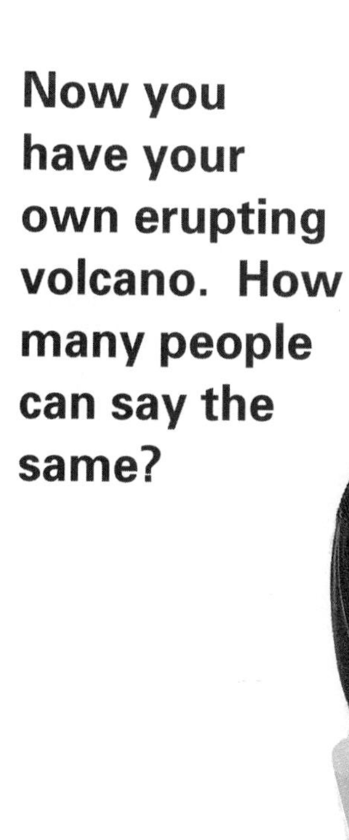

Now you have your own erupting volcano. How many people can say the same?

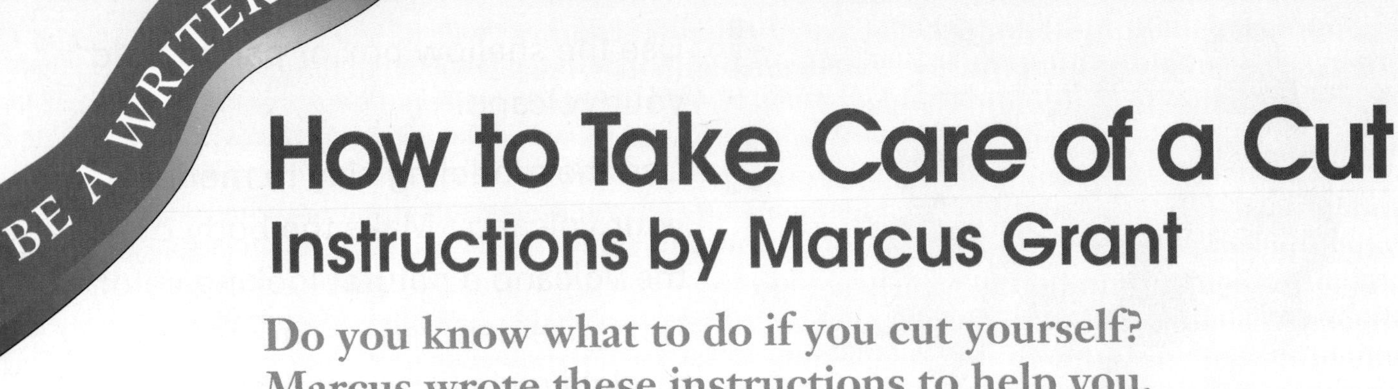

How to Take Care of a Cut

Instructions by Marcus Grant

Do you know what to do if you cut yourself? Marcus wrote these instructions to help you.

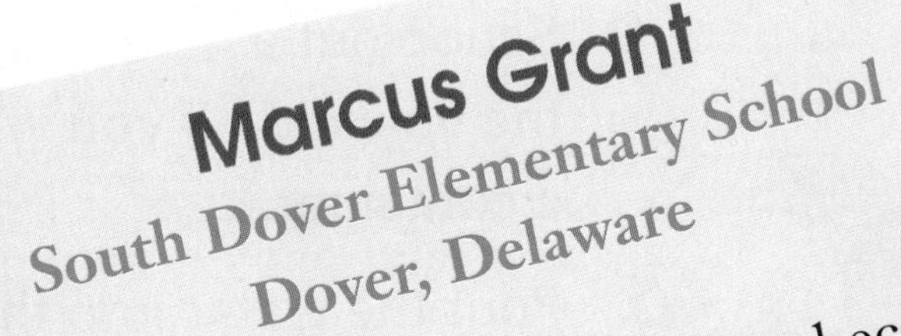

Marcus Grant

South Dover Elementary School
Dover, Delaware

Marcus says that he likes to write because "I get to share my ideas." His favorite writing topic is sports, but he often gets ideas for writing from the books he reads.

Marcus likes to play football and basketball and ride his bike. When he grows up, Marcus would like to be a singer.

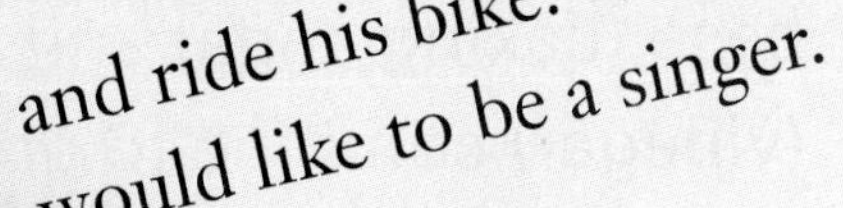

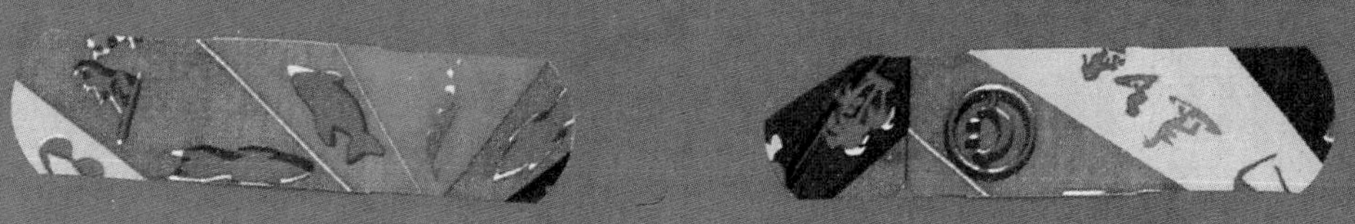

How to Take Care of a Cut

Here is what to do if you get a cut. First, you should stay calm. Second, let your mom or another adult see the cut. Third, clean off your cut with a clean cloth, soap, and water. If the cut is still bleeding after you clean it, hold a clean cloth on it and put pressure on it to make it stop bleeding.

Next, after the bleeding has stopped, put a bandage on it so the cut can heal. When you put the bandage on, don't touch the gauze in the middle because that is the important part. If that part gets dirty, your cut will get dirty too.

After the cut has healed, take the bandage off so that the cut can have air. Finally, if the cut doesn't heal, go to the doctor to see if it's infected.

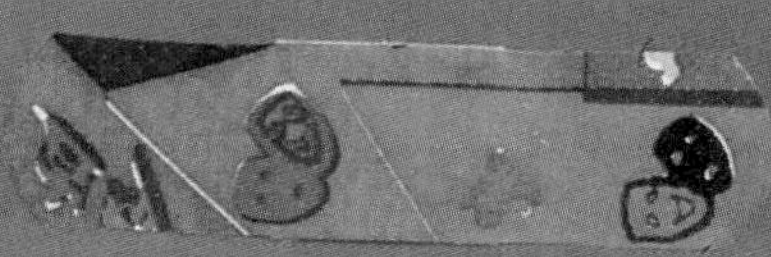

Meet the Author
Marjorie Stover

Marjorie Stover's grandparents were pioneers who moved to Nebraska in the 1800s. Today, Stover's home in Nebraska is filled with furniture and other things her family carried West in a covered wagon. Stover enjoys writing historical books — and baking molasses cookies!

Meet the Illustrator
Brad Teare

What would it be like to live alone in a log cabin in the middle of a forest without running water or electricity? Brad Teare knows, because he once lived that way for a year in Idaho. Teare now lives in Utah — in a home with both running water and electricity.

PATRICK AND THE GREAT MOLASSES EXPLOSION

by Marjorie Stover

There once was a boy named Patrick McGonnigal O'Brien. He had red hair and freckles, and he lived with his mama, his papa, and his two-year-old sister, Mary, in the city of Boston.

Now if there was one thing in this wide world that Patrick had a fondness and a craving for, it was molasses. He had molasses on his oatmeal for breakfast. He had molasses on his pancakes for lunch. For supper he had Boston brown bread and baked beans sweetened with molasses.

Still, Patrick had never had enough molasses to satisfy his craving. He was always trying to get another lick. When Mama filled the molasses pitcher from the tin pail, he was right there to run his finger along the edge and lick up the dribbles.

One day when Mama's back was turned, Patrick stuck his finger into the pitcher to sneak a lick. In his hurry he tipped the pitcher over! Mama turned around just as the molasses poured out in a gooey, brown puddle on the tablecloth.

"Patrick McGonnigal O'Brien! See what you've done!" scolded Mama. The red bun of hair on the back of her head waggled from side to side. She scraped up the molasses with a spoon, but not one drop did Patrick get.

Every Sunday afternoon Papa took Patrick for a walk down along the harbor to see all the wonderful sights. Horses and buggies clattered over the cobblestones. New-fangled automobiles tooted their horns. Overhead, a train clacked along the raised tracks.

In the harbor they saw all kinds of boats — freighters, steamboats, tugboats, and sailboats. Together they stood on a freight-loading platform where Papa worked on weekdays. Patrick liked to brag that Papa could load and unload boxes and barrels as fast as the fastest man there, and maybe a wee bit faster.

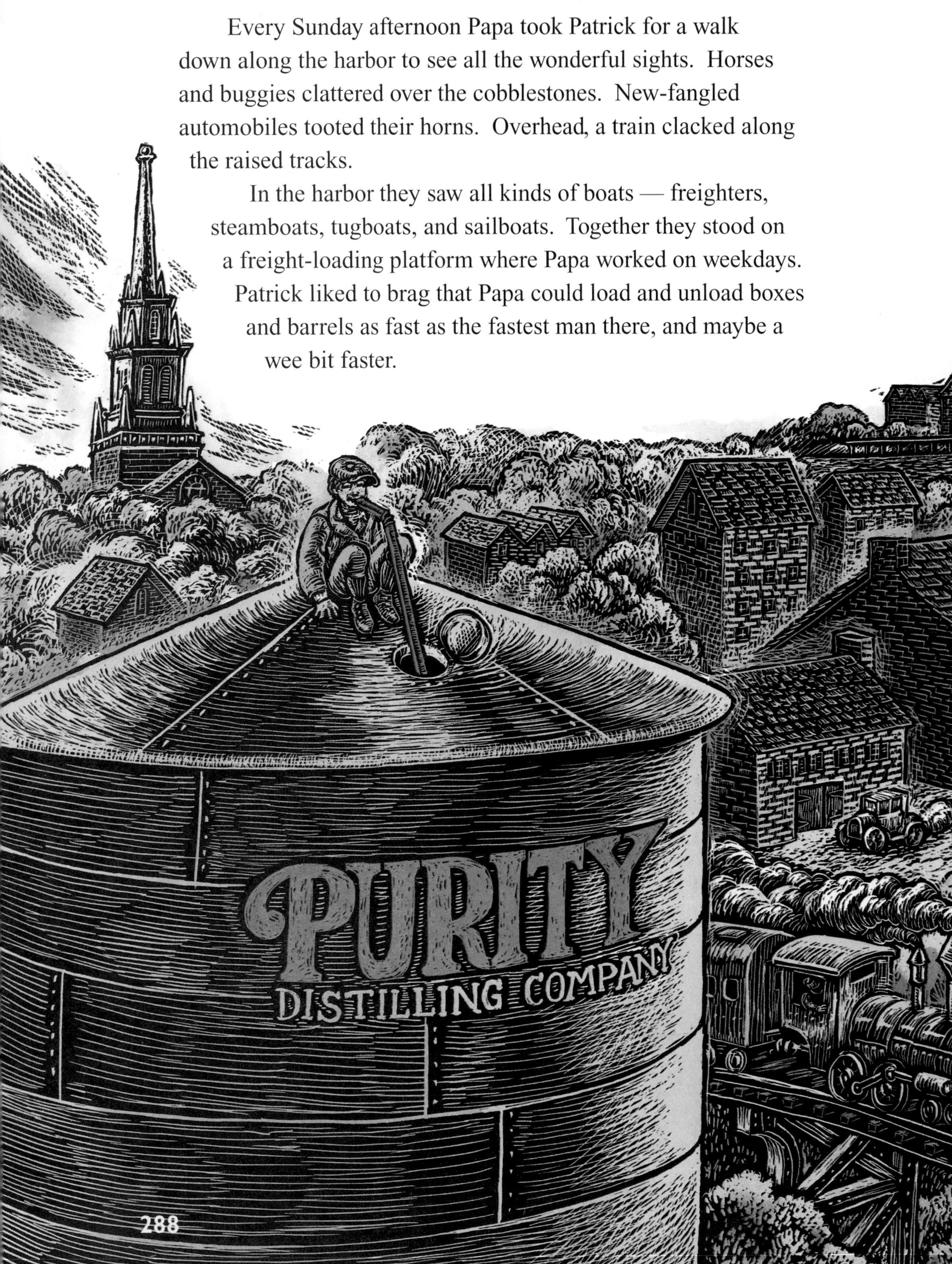

They always stopped in the stable to see the big Belgian work horses that pulled the heavy freight wagons. Now and then Patrick slipped a sugar lump to one of the horses. Papa teased Patrick that the horses liked sugar as much as Patrick liked molasses.

The most wonderful sight of all, however, was a huge, enormous tank as tall as a four-story building. The tank was made of big sheets of metal fastened together with rivets. Patrick could see the large, round heads of the rivets pounded in neat rows along the seams. Painted in big letters on the round sides of the tank were the words, PURITY DISTILLING COMPANY. This giant tank was filled with molasses. Papa had said so.

The very thought of so much molasses made Patrick's mouth water. Sometimes Patrick dreamed that he was seated on the edge of the tank with a giant straw just sucking, sucking, sucking molasses all day long.

One winter day when Patrick arrived home from school for lunch, Mama said, "Eat your soup and crackers, and don't delay. I've a fancy to make oatmeal molasses cookies this afternoon, but the molasses pail is empty. If you hurry, you can get it filled at the corner store before you go back to school."

At the thought of molasses cookies, Patrick's green eyes twinkled. He slurped down his soup as fast as he could. He pulled on his cap, buttoned his jacket, and hooked the wire handle of the empty pail over his fingers.

"Now mind," said Mama, "don't you dare stick your finger in for a lick, or not a single molasses cookie will you have."

The sun was shining, and it was not a very cold day for the middle of January. Patrick ran as fast as he could to Mr. O'Connor's store.

When the storekeeper saw Patrick swinging the molasses pail, he shook his bald head. "Sorry I am to disappoint you, lad, but the molasses barrel is empty. I'm getting a new barrel this afternoon. Come back after school, and I'll fill your pail."

Patrick walked slowly out of the store. His mouth was watering for molasses cookies hot from the oven. Then he had an idea. A few blocks farther on was another store — a bigger store. He had never gone there by himself, but he and Papa often passed it on their Sunday walks. The store was near the corner where they turned onto Commercial Street.

He did not have time to go home and ask Mama, but Patrick was sure he could get the molasses and not be late for school. Holding tight to the wire handle, Patrick ran lickety-split. He ran so hard that when he reached the store, he stopped on the doorstep to catch his breath.

At that very moment a heavy rumbling sound filled the air. BANG! BANG! BANG! BOOM! BOOM! WH-O-O-O-O-O-SH!

Patrick rushed to the corner. What he saw made his eyes bulge. A great, towering wave of smooth, shiny brown rolled toward him. It looked like . . . it looked like . . . IT WAS MOLASSES!

The Purity Distilling Company's huge, enormous tank had E-X-P-L-O-D-E-D!

People covered with molasses ran in all directions. People with their feet stuck fast screamed for help. Horses struggled in the sticky mess. Above all the noise and chaos, three long alarms sounded loudly through the streets.

All the while the river of molasses rolled toward Patrick. Without stopping to think, he bent down by the corner of the building. Grabbing the lid off his pail, he held it out. The molasses poured into the pail, nearly jerking it from Patrick's hands. He pulled it back and clapped on the lid. The molasses spread up the side street and lapped around Patrick's shoes.

Patrick turned to run, but he lost his footing in the gooey river. Down he went, his hand held tightly onto the pail. As he rolled over, a hand grabbed him.

"Are you all right, boy?" A man with hair as red as Patrick's smiled down at him. Strong hands pulled him to his feet.

Patrick nodded as he wiped his sticky face with a sticky hand. Before he could even say thank you, the man was

gone. Patrick's shoes, his pants, his jacket, and his cap dripped with molasses. Patrick stamped off, stick — unstick, stick — unstick.

The terribly sweet smell of molasses filled the air. Around him men shouted, women screamed, and horses neighed. Behind him buildings crashed.

Patrick, however, did not look back. He was too busy licking molasses. Lick-lick. He licked first one hand and then the other. Women called to him from their doorsteps. Patrick did not answer. With his thumb, Patrick wiped the molasses from his face. Lick-lick. He walked slowly on, the pail of molasses dangling from one hand. Stick — unstick, lick-lick. Stick — unstick, lick-lick.

Patrick ran his thumb over his jacket. Lick-lick. As he made his way home, Patrick became worried. Not only would Mama think he had taken a lick, but he was going to be late for school. Patrick knew he was in big trouble.

As Patrick started up the back walk, the kitchen door flew open. Mama stared at him. "Patrick McGonnigal O'Brien! What have you done to yourself?"

"I . . . I fell in the molasses, Mama." He gave his fingers a quick lick.

"What do you mean? 'Fell in the molasses.' You look as if you had climbed into Mr. O'Connor's barrel and licked it clean!" The red bun on Mama's head waggled back and forth.

Patrick shook his head. "Mr. O'Connor's barrel was empty, so I ran to the store near the corner of Commercial Street. Then I heard a terrible noise. BANG! BANG! BANG! BOOM! BOOM! WH-O-O-O-O-SH!" Patrick waved a sticky fist in the air.

"I ran to look. What do you think? The Purity Distilling Company's great big tank of molasses had popped open! The molasses rolled down the street right at me. I filled my pail and came home as fast as I could."

Mama's face turned bright red. "Patrick McGonnigal O'Brien! 'Tis bad enough that you are covered with molasses and late for school. Now you make matters worse by telling the silliest lie I ever heard!"

"It's true, Mama, every word!" cried Patrick. "I held out my bucket and filled it in the molasses river. If I hadn't fallen down . . ."

Mama grabbed him by the ear. "I never saw such a sticky mess nor heard such a tall tale. Come along and not another word out of you."

"But Mama . . ." Patrick cried.

"Patrick, I will hear no more stories, and I don't want you waking little Mary. I've had my hands full today already with your sister bumping her head and crying enough tears to make a flood."

"But Mama, there was a flood. A molasses flood."

"Patrick!"

Patrick sat in the big washtub in the middle of the kitchen floor. Every Saturday night he took his bath in it. This was not Saturday, but he was having a bath.

Mama's hands were not very gentle as she washed his hair and his neck and ears. "My goodness! There's even molasses on the back of your head. How did you ever get into such a sticky mess?"

Patrick tried again. " 'Tis like I told you. The big tank of molasses over by Commercial Street . . ."

Mama's eyes flashed like green lightning. "No more of that!" she scolded and rubbed him dry with a rough towel. She handed him his nightshirt. "It's into bed with you, and there you'll stay until you're ready to tell the truth."

Patrick opened his mouth and then shut it again. Mama was angrier than he had ever seen her. Angrier than the day he had spilled the molasses pitcher on the table. Patrick shook his head. He had told the truth, and she wouldn't believe him. Sadly he crawled into bed.

“Mind, when you’re ready to tell what really happened, you can come out,” said Mama as she closed the door.

Patrick pulled the covers up tight. He felt terrible. What could he say? He shut his eyes to think better. Soon he was fast asleep.

When Patrick awoke, he could smell supper cooking. He was hungry, but Mama had said . . . He rubbed his red hair. He would try again. He would start at the beginning and explain very slowly the way his teacher did. Patrick slid out of bed and tiptoed into the kitchen.

Mama was sitting at the table feeding Mary her porridge. Patrick stared at his sister. She had a bump on her forehead, half the size of a hen's egg.

Mama looked at him sternly. "Are you ready to tell me what really happened?" she asked.

Patrick swallowed hard and nodded. "I took the molasses pail and went to Mr. O'Connor's store, just like you told me to do, Mama. But Mr. O'Connor's molasses barrel was empty." He took a deep breath. "So, I ran as fast as I could to the store near the corner of Commercial Street. I was sure I could fill my pail and not be late for school. Only . . . only . . ."

Patrick shook his head. He suddenly realized that if he had not seen that flood of molasses, he would not have believed it himself.

"Only what?" insisted Mama.

Patrick looked hard at his mother. "Mama, what would make a great big tank like that pop open?"

Mama shook her head. "It couldn't! That's why your story is so silly."

"But if it did," Patrick continued, "think what an awful mess it would make. Horses and people would get stuck in the molasses."

"Patrick, stop pretending, and tell me how you got in such a mess. Papa will soon be home, and . . ."

“Papa! I forgot about Papa!” Patrick’s face turned white beneath his freckles. “I wonder where Papa was!”

“Papa? Papa’s at . . . ” Mama stopped short. Before she could say another word, the kitchen door opened, and Papa stepped in. At least Patrick thought it was Papa. From head to foot he was streaked with molasses. His face and hands were copper colored, and his black hair and his clothes were all sticky. Papa closed the door behind him, and the heavy sweet smell of molasses filled the kitchen.

Mama gave a loud cry.

Papa stood there, trying to wipe a sticky hand on his sticky trousers. “Did you hear what happened?” he asked.

Mama just stared, as if she could not believe her eyes.

“The Purity Distilling Company tank exploded,” said Papa, “and the tank was filled to the very top. Two million, three hundred and sixty thousand gallons of molasses poured out over the people, the buildings, and the streets.”

Mama gasped, and her green eyes opened wider.

“I was sitting on the loading dock, eating my lunch,” Papa went on. “All of a sudden I heard this terrible rumbling and shots that sounded like a giant machine gun being fired. Only it wasn’t a gun. The rivets that hold the molasses tank together popped off like buttons off my jacket. The next thing I knew, one side of the tank had blown clear into the North Side Park. Fourteen thousand tons of molasses poured out, covering everything in its path — people, horses, wagons, cars, buildings, and even a piece of the raised train track.”

Patrick looked at Mama. Would she tell Papa she didn't believe him and send him to bed? No. Mama was speechless.

Papa stuck out a sticky shoe. "Have you ever tried walking through molasses? It flowed into buildings and flooded basements. I worked all afternoon helping people and horses get unstuck. People from all over the city helped."

Papa rubbed a sticky ear. "It's a wonder you didn't hear the explosion way up here."

Mama shook her head weakly. "Oh dear, that must have been when Mary bumped her head. She set up such a howl." Mama looked from Papa to Patrick. "To think I wouldn't believe . . . Oh, Patrick, my boy! If you like, you can pour molasses all over your supper tonight."

Patrick drew a deep breath. The heavy smell of molasses filled his nose with a sickening sweetness. His tummy felt strange. "Thank you, Mama, but for once I've had all the molasses I want."

Sticking to the Story

Write a Story

You Get Your Wish

Patrick loved molasses. What is *your* favorite food? Spaghetti? French fries? Invent a story about an unusual event in your town that allows you to get as much of your favorite food as you want.

Create a News Report

Travel Back in Time

Work with a group to create a live news report from the scene of the great molasses explosion. You'll need someone to play a television reporter, while others can be Patrick, his father, and other witnesses.

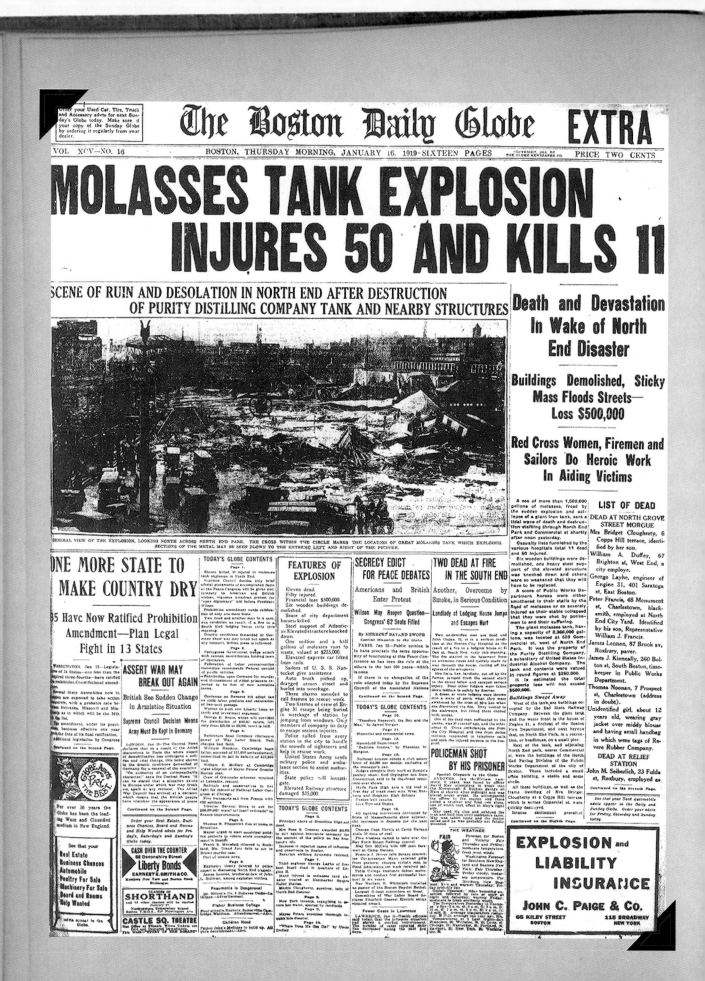

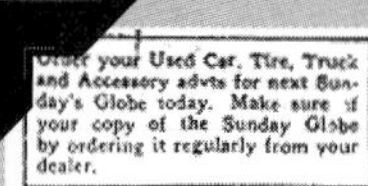

The Boston Daily Globe EXTRA

VOL XCV—NO. 16 BOSTON, THURSDAY MORNING, JANUARY 16, 1919—SIXTEEN PAGES COPYRIGHT, 1919, BY THE GLOBE NEWSPAPER CO. PRICE TWO CENTS

MOLASSES TANK EXPLOSION INJURES 50 AND KILLS 11

SCENE OF RUIN AND DESOLATION IN NORTH END AFTER DESTRUCTION OF PURITY DISTILLING COMPANY TANK AND NEARBY STRUCTURES

GENERAL VIEW OF THE EXPLOSION, LOOKING NORTH ACROSS NORTH END PARK. THE CROSS WITHIN THE CIRCLE MARKS THE LOCATION OF GREAT MOLASSES TANK WHICH EXPLODED. SECTIONS OF THE METAL MAY BE SEEN BLOWN TO THE EXTREME LEFT AND RIGHT OF THE PICTURE.

Death and Devastation In Wake of North End Disaster

Buildings Demolished, Sticky Mass Floods Streets—Loss $500,000

Red Cross Women, Firemen and Sailors Do Heroic Work In Aiding Victims

A sea of more than 1,500,000 gallons of molasses, freed by the sudden explosion and collapse of a giant iron tank, sent a tidal wave of death and destruction stalking through North End Park and Commercial st shortly after noon yesterday.

Casualty lists furnished by the various hospitals total 11 dead and 50 injured.

Six wooden buildings were demolished, one heavy steel support of the elevated structure was knocked down and others were so weakened that they will have to be replaced.

A score of Public Works Department horses were either smothered in their stalls by the flood of molasses or so severely injured as their stable collapsed that they were shot by policemen to end their suffering.

The giant molasses tank, having a capacity of 2,360,000 gallons, was located at 529 Commercial st, west of North End Park. It was the property of the Purity Distilling Company, a subsidiary of United States Industrial Alcohol Company. The tank and contents were valued in round figures at $250,000.

It is estimated the total property loss will not exceed $500,000.

Buildings Swept Away

West of the tank are buildings occupied by the Bay State Railway Company. Between the giant tank and the water front is the house of Engine 31, a fireboat of the Boston Fire Department, and next beyond that, on North End Park, is a recreation, or headhouse, on a small pier.

East of the tank, and adjoining North End park, nearer Commercial st, were the buildings of the North End Paving Division of the Public Works Department of the city of Boston. These included a small office building, a stable and some sheds.

All these buildings, as well as the frame dwelling of Mrs Bridget Clougherty at 6 Copps Hill terrace which is across Commercial st, were quickly destroyed.

Intense excitement prevailed

Continued on the Eighth Page.

LIST OF DEAD

DEAD AT NORTH GROVE STREET MORGUE

Mrs Bridget Clougherty, 6 Copps Hill terrace, identified by her son.

William A. Duffey, 67 Brighton st, West End, a city employe.

George Layhe, engineer of Engine 31, 401 Saratoga st, East Boston.

Peter Francis, 48 Monument st, Charlestown, blacksmith, employed at North End City Yard. Identified by his son, Representative William J. Francis.

James Lennon, 87 Brook av, Roxbury, paver.

James J. Kinneally, 260 Bolton st, South Boston, timekeeper in Public Works Department.

Thomas Noonan, 7 Prospect st, Charlestown (address in doubt).

Unidentified girl, about 12 years old, wearing gray jacket over middy blouse and having small handbag in which were tags of Revere Rubber Company.

DEAD AT RELIEF STATION

John M. Seiberlich, 23 Fulda st, Roxbury, employed as

Continued on the Seventh Page.

See that your Used Automobile advts appear in the Daily and Sunday Globe. Order your advts for Friday, Saturday and Sunday today.

ONE MORE STATE TO MAKE COUNTRY DRY

35 Have Now Ratified Prohibition Amendment—Plan Legal Fight in 13 States

WASHINGTON, Jan 15—Legislatures of 35 States—one less than the required three-fourths—have ratified the prohibition Constitutional amendment.

Several State Assemblies now in session are expected to take action tomorrow, with a probable race between Nebraska, Missouri and Minnesota as to which will be the 36th on the list.

The amendment, under its provisions, becomes effective one year from the date of its final ratification.

Additional legislation by Congress

Continued on the Second Page.

ASSERT WAR MAY BREAK OUT AGAIN

British See Sudden Change in Armistice Situation

Supreme Council Decision Means Army Must Be Kept in Germany

LONDON, Jan 15—The Central News declares that as a result of the Allied discussions in Paris the whole aspect of demobilization has undergone a sudden and vital change, this being shown in the drastic conditions demanded of Germany for a renewal of the armistice.

"On authority of an unimpeachable character," says the Central News, "it can be stated that a situation exists in Europe under which war may break out again at any moment. The Allied War Council has arrived at a decision which means that the British people have mistaken the appearance of peace

Continued on the Second Page.

TODAY'S GLOBE CONTENTS

FEATURES OF EXPLOSION

Eleven dead.
Fifty injured.
Financial loss $500,000.
Six wooden buildings demolished.
Score of city department horses killed.
Steel support of Atlantic-av Elevated structure knocked down.
One million and a half gallons of molasses runs to waste, valued at $225,000.
Elevated express car lifted from rails.
Sailors of U. S. S. Nantucket give assistance.
Auto truck picked up, dragged across street and hurled into wreckage.
Three alarms sounded to call firemen to rescue work.
Two firemen of crew of Engine 31 escape being buried in wreckage of station by jumping from windows. Only members of company on duty to escape serious injuries.
Police called from every station in the city to handle the crowds of sightseers and help in rescue work.
United States Army sends military police and ambulance section to assist authorities.
State police will investigate.
Elevated Railway structure damaged $35,000.

TODAY'S GLOBE CONTENTS

SECRECY EDICT FOR PEACE DEBATES

Americans and British Enter Protest

Wilson May Reopen Question—Congress' 62 Seats Filled

By HERBERT BAYARD SWOPE
Special Dispatch to the Globe

PARIS, Jan 15—Public opinion is to have precisely the same opportunity of functioning at this Peace Conference as has been the rule at the others in the last 300 years—which is none.

If there is no abrogation of the rule adopted today by the Supreme Council of the Associated Nations

Continued on the Second Page.

TODAY'S GLOBE CONTENTS

TWO DEAD AT FIRE IN THE SOUTH END

Another, Overcome by Smoke, in Serious Condition

Landlady of Lodging House Jumps and Escapes Hurt

Two unidentified men are dead and John Cagan, 33, is in a serious condition at the Boston City Hospital as the result of a fire in a lodging house at 15 Oak st, South End, early this morning. The fire started in the basement from an unknown cause and quickly made its way through the house, cutting off the egress of the occupants.

Mrs Delia Lee, landlady, cut off by the flames, jumped from the second story to the street below and escaped serious injury. Four other lodgers were taken down ladders to safety by firemen.

A dozen or more lodgers were thrown into a state of panic when they were awakened by the cries of Mrs Lee when she discovered the fire. They rushed to the stairways, but found them choked with smoke.

One of the dead men, suffocated by the smoke, was 30 years of age, and the other about 45. Three ambulances, one from the City Hospital and two from police stations, responded to telephone calls and took the injured persons to the hospital.

POLICEMAN SHOT BY HIS PRISONER

Special Dispatch to the Globe

ANDOVER, Jan 16—William Lawrence, 11 years, was found by officer David Kay attempting to break into the Wyncoogh & Buchan garage on Main st shortly after midnight and was placed under arrest. He accompanied the officer to the station and there pulled a revolver and fired two shots, one of which took effect in May's right side.

May used his club and subdued the man and held him until assistance came. May was taken home and the doctor called said he was probably not fatally wounded.

THE WEATHER

FAIR

Forecast for Boston and Vicinity: Fair Thursday and Friday; moderate temperature, fresh west winds.

Washington Forecast for Southern New England and Eastern New York: Fair Thursday; Friday cloudy, moderate temperature. For Northern New England: Fair and warmer Thursday; Friday...

It Really Happened

by Marjorie Stover

A piece of the metal tank on Commercial Street after the explosion

Oldtimers in Boston say that to this very day you can smell a faint whiff of molasses in the old buildings on Commercial Street. But is that only an oldtimer's tall tale?

The truth, as Patrick's mother would want to have it told, is that on January 15, 1919, a giant storage tank on Commercial Street in Boston's North End exploded. The tank, built by the Purity Distilling Company four years before, was filled with molasses, over 2,000,000 gallons.

The molasses storage tank before the explosion

Many buildings were heavily damaged by the flood.

When the tank popped, a great brown wave of molasses flooded downtown Boston, sweeping over everything in its path. In some places the molasses was three feet deep. Children on their lunch break from school were knocked over. Pieces of the tank flew in all directions, and one flying chunk of metal is reported to have crashed into the nearby freight house. Houses collapsed under the flood of molasses, and several people as well as horses were killed.

Rescue workers, trucks, and equipment had a difficult time getting through the streets of gooey liquid. Cleanup crews were brought in, but their task seemed almost impossible. Everywhere people walked and everything they touched was sticky. Before the great flood ended, 21 people had been killed and 150 injured.

Even after the last brown glob disappeared from Commercial Street, the smell of molasses remained in Boston for a long time. Whether you can still sniff the molasses where it soaked into the cracks and crannies and under the wooden boards back in 1919, you will need to go to Boston and discover for yourself.

Following the explosion, the streets of Boston were coated with molasses.

GLOSSARY

Some of the words in this book may have pronunciations or meanings you do not know. This glossary can help you by telling you how to pronounce those words and by telling you the meanings for the words as they are used in this book.

You can find out how to pronounce any glossary word by using the special spelling after the word and the key that runs across the bottom of the glossary pages.

The full pronunciation key on the next page shows how to pronounce each consonant and vowel in a special spelling. The pronunciation key at the bottom of the glossary pages is a shortened form of the full key.

Full Pronunciation Key

Consonant Sounds

b	**b**i**b**, ca**bb**age	kw	**ch**oir, **qu**ick	t	**t**igh**t**, stopp**ed**
ch	**ch**ur**ch**, sti**tch**	l	**l**id, need**le**, ta**ll**	th	ba**th**, **th**in
d	**d**ee**d**, mail**ed**, pu**dd**le	m	a**m**, **m**an, du**mb**	*th*	ba**th**e, **th**is
f	**f**ast, **f**i**f**e, o**ff**, **ph**rase, rou**gh**	n	**n**o, sudd**en**	v	ca**v**e, val**v**e, **v**ine
g	**g**a**g**, **g**et, fin**g**er	ng	thi**ng**, i**n**k	w	**w**ith, **w**olf
h	**h**at, **wh**o	p	**p**o**p**, ha**pp**y	y	**y**es, **y**olk, on**i**on
hw	**wh**ich, **wh**ere	r	**r**oa**r**, **rh**yme	z	ro**s**e, si**z**e, **x**ylophone, **z**ebra
j	**j**u**dg**e, **g**em	s	mi**ss**, **s**au**c**e, **sc**ene, **s**ee	zh	gara**g**e, plea**s**ure, vi**s**ion
k	**c**at, **k**i**ck**, s**ch**ool	sh	di**sh**, **sh**ip, **s**ugar, ti**ss**ue		

Vowel Sounds

ă	r**a**t, l**au**gh	ŏ	h**o**rrible, p**o**t	ŭ	c**u**t, fl**oo**d, r**ou**gh, s**o**me
ā	**a**pe, **ai**d, p**ay**	ō	g**o**, r**ow**, t**oe**, th**ough**	û	c**i**rcle, f**u**r, h**ea**rd, t**e**rm, t**u**rn, **u**rge, w**o**rd
â	**ai**r, c**a**re, w**ea**r	ô	**a**ll, c**au**ght, f**o**r, p**aw**	yo͝o	c**u**re
ä	f**a**ther, koal**a**, y**a**rd	oi	b**oy**, n**oi**se, **oi**l	yo͞o	ab**u**se, **u**se
ĕ	p**e**t, pl**ea**sure, **a**ny	ou	c**ow**, **ou**t	ə	**a**bout, sil**e**nt, penc**i**l, lem**o**n, circ**u**s
ē	b**e**, b**ee**, **ea**sy, p**i**ano	o͝o	f**u**ll, t**oo**k, w**o**lf		
ĭ	**i**f, p**i**t, b**u**sy	o͞o	b**oo**t, fr**ui**t, fl**ew**		
ī	b**y**, p**ie**, h**igh**				
î	d**ea**r, d**ee**r, f**ie**rce, m**e**re				

Stress Marks

Primary Stress **ʹ**: bi•ol•o•gy [bī **ŏlʹ** ə jē]

Secondary Stress ʹ: bi•o•log•i•cal [bīʹ ə **lŏjʹ** i kəl]

A

ac•cent (**ăk**′ sĕnt′) *noun* A small detail that looks different from the things around it, usually added for color or decoration: *The bedroom was blue with pink pillows for **accent**.*

a•do•be (ə **dō**′ bē) *noun* Brick that is made from clay and straw and dried in the sun: *Many houses in the southwestern United States are built with **adobe**.*

adobe

ADOBE

Adobe is a Spanish word. It goes back to the Arabic word *attoba* meaning "the brick."

an•xious•ly (**ăngk**′ shəs lē′) *adverb* In a worried way: *The crowd watched **anxiously** as the firefighter carried the child down the ladder.*

art•ist (**är**′ tĭst) *noun* **1.** A person who practices an art, such as painting or music: *The **artist** displayed her paintings in the town hall.* **2.** A person who shows great skill in what he or she does: *Mr. Brown's bake shop has the prettiest wedding cakes in town. He is a true **artist**.*

B

bar•rel (**băr**′ əl) *noun* A large, round container with a flat top and bottom: *On the ship, fresh water was stored in large wooden **barrels**.*

barrels

bel•low (**bĕl**′ ō) *verb* To say in a deep, loud voice: *The police officer **bellowed** to the crowd to get away from the burning building.*

brace (brās) *verb* To get ready for something difficult or unpleasant: *As Eric walked toward the lake, he **braced** himself against the shock of the cold water.*

ă r**a**t / ā p**ay** / â c**a**re / ä f**a**ther / ĕ p**e**t / ē b**e** / ĭ p**i**t / ī p**ie** / î f**ie**rce / ŏ p**o**t / ō g**o** / ô p**aw**, f**o**r / oi **oi**l / o͝o t**oo**k

bur•y (**bĕr**´ ē) *verb* To hide or cover by placing under the ground: *The wind blew sand over the beach and **buried** my sandals.*

C

cac•tus (**kăk**´ təs) *noun* A plant with thick, often spiny, leafless stems that grows in hot, dry places.

cactus

crav•ing (**krā**´ vĭng) *noun* A very strong desire for something: *As I passed the bakery, I suddenly had a **craving** for a piece of apple pie.*

cus•tom (**kŭs**´ təm) *noun* Something that members of a group usually do: *One birthday **custom** is to blow out the candles on a birthday cake.*

D

des•ert (**dĕz**´ ərt) *noun* A dry area of land that is usually sandy and without trees: *Very few plants grow in the **desert** because it hardly ever rains.*

> **DESERT**
>
> *Desert* comes from a Latin word meaning "to abandon, or leave behind." When a place was abandoned, it was called a *desert*.

de•sign (dĭ **zīn**´) *noun* A pleasing pattern of lines and shapes: *The wrapping paper was decorated with colorful flower and leaf **designs**.*

di•a•mond (**dī**´ ə mənd) *noun* A shape (◊) with four equal sides.

dust storm (dŭst stôrm) *noun* Strong winds that carry clouds of sand and dust across an area: *During the **dust storm**, Dad had to stop the car because he couldn't see to drive.*

E

e•rupt (ĭ **rŭpt**´) *verb* To burst out violently: *The moving van knocked over the fire hydrant, and water **erupted** into the air.*

o͞o b**oo**t / ou **ou**t / ŭ c**u**t / û f**u**r / hw **wh**ich / th **th**in / *th* **th**is / zh vi**s**ion / ə **a**bout, sil**e**nt, penc**i**l, lem**o**n, circ**u**s

F

fu•ri•ous (**fyo͝or′** ē əs) *adjective* Full of anger: *Carlos was **furious** when he saw that the puppy had chewed his favorite shoes.*

G

gas (găs) *noun* A poisonous substance that is not liquid or solid and fills the air: *The instructions for the new stove said to call for repairs right away if we smelled **gas**.*

goo•ey (**go͞o′** ē) *adjective* Very sticky: *The jar of honey fell off the table and broke into a **gooey** mess on the floor.*

> **GOOEY**
> *Gooey* is the adjective form of the noun *goo,* which, in turn, may come from the word *burgoo*. *Burgoo* was a thick kind of oatmeal served to sailors long ago.

grunt (grŭnt) *verb* To say or speak in a short, deep, harsh voice: *Grandpa sleepily **grunted** an answer to my question.*

I

in•spire (ĭn **spīr′**) *verb* To cause someone to think or act in a particular way: *My grandmother, who made all of her own clothes, **inspired** me to learn to sew.*

mar•ket (**mär′** kĭt) *noun* A place where people buy and sell goods: *Mr. Choy goes to the **market** each morning to buy fresh fish for his restaurant.*

market

ă rat / ā pay / â care / ä father / ĕ pet / ē be / ĭ pit / ī pie / î fierce / ŏ pot / ō go / ô paw, for / oi oil / o͝o took

mo•las•ses (mə **lăs′** ĭz) *noun* A thick, sweet syrup: *Marta likes to put **molasses** on her pancakes.*

MOLASSES
Molasses comes from the Portuguese word *melaço*, which means "honey."

or•ders (**ôr′** dərz) *noun* Certain commands or rules that must be followed: *A soldier must follow the commander's **orders**.*

pang (păng) *noun* A short but sharp feeling, as of pain: *Just before dinner, I began having little **pangs** of hunger.*

pas•sen•ger (**păs′** ən jər) *noun* A person riding in a vehicle, such as a car, a plane, or a boat: *All the **passengers** in our car must wear their seat belts.*

passengers

pitch•er (**pĭch′** ər) *noun* A container, usually with a handle, for holding and pouring liquids: *Mom placed a **pitcher** of cold milk on the table.*

plot (plŏt) *verb* To plan secretly: *Dad will **plot** a way to sneak Mom's birthday present into the house without her seeing it.*

poi•son•ous (**poi′** zə nəs) *adjective* Causing sickness or death when swallowed or breathed: *The firefighter had to wear a mask to protect him from the **poisonous** air.*

prowl (proul) *verb* To sneak about as if hunting or looking for something: *The stray dog was **prowling** the streets looking for food.*

o͞o b**oo**t / ou **ou**t / ŭ c**u**t / û f**u**r / hw **wh**ich / th **th**in / *th* **th**is / zh vi**s**ion / ə **a**bout, sil**e**nt, penc**i**l, lem**o**n, circ**u**s

pyr•a•mid (**pĭr′** ə mĭd) *noun* A figure that has a flat bottom and sides shaped like triangles.

pyramid

R

rec•og•nize (**rĕk′** əg nīz′) *verb* To see and know from past experience: *Even from far away, Becky could **recognize** her brother in the crowd by his red cowboy hat.*

res•cue (**rĕs′** kyo͞o) *adjective* Being able to save from danger or harm: *The **rescue** team hurried up the mountain to help the hurt hiker.*

scene (sēn) *noun* A view of a place: *The photograph showed a **scene** of a cabin by a lake.*

scheme (skēm) *verb* To make up a plan for: *Our team will **scheme** to win the game.*

sur•vi•vor (sər **vī′** vər) *noun* Someone who manages to stay alive: *All the **survivors** of the car accident had been wearing seat belts.*

T

tat•tered (**tăt′** ərd) *adjective* Torn and ragged looking: *By the time Andy got the stuffed animal away from the puppy, it was torn and **tattered**.*

> **TATTERED**
>
> *Tattered* comes from the Scandinavian word *tötturr*, which means "rag."

ti•tle (**tīt′** l) *noun* A name given to a person to show rank, office, or job: *After finishing medical school, my uncle's new **title** became* Doctor.

ti•tle fight (**tīt′** l fīt) *noun* A boxing match to determine the champion: *Joe Louis first won the heavyweight championship in a **title fight** in 1937.*

ă r**a**t / ā p**ay** / â c**a**re / ä f**a**ther / ĕ p**e**t / ē b**e** / ĭ p**i**t / ī p**ie** / î f**ie**rce / ŏ p**o**t / ō g**o** / ô p**aw,** f**o**r / oi **oi**l / o͝o t**oo**k

trem•ble (**trĕm´** bəl) *verb* **1.** To shake from fear or the cold: *I knew Aunt Shirley was afraid of something when I saw her hands* ***trembling****.* **2.** To shake: *The earthquake made our house* ***tremble****.*

tri•an•gle (**trī´** ăng´ gəl) A shape (Δ) with three sides.

tum•ble•weed (**tŭm´** bəl wēd´) *noun* A plant that breaks off from its roots when it dies and is blown about in the wind.

tumbleweed

vol•ca•no (vŏl **kā´** nō) *noun* An opening in the earth through which lava, ash, and hot gases come out.

volcano

VOLCANO

Volcano comes from the Latin word *Vulcanus* and the name of a god in Roman mythology. In these myths, *Vulcan*, "the god of fire," was thought to cause volcanoes.

voy•age (**voi´** ĭj) A long trip to a far away place: *The Wu family took a long* ***voyage*** *across the Pacific Ocean when they moved to the United States.*

whirl (wûrl) *verb* To spin around in circles: *The children* ***whirled*** *round and round until they felt dizzy.*

whirl•wind (**wûrl´** wĭnd´) *noun* A current of air that spins rapidly around: *The* ***whirlwind*** *picked up the pile of leaves and spun them around in circles.*

o͞o b**oo**t / ou **ou**t / ŭ c**u**t / û f**ur** / hw **wh**ich / th **th**in / *th* **th**is / zh vi**s**ion / ə **a**bout, sil**e**nt, penc**i**l, lem**o**n, circ**u**s

ACKNOWLEDGMENTS

For each of the selections listed below, grateful acknowledgment is made for permission to excerpt and/or reprint original or copyrighted material, as follows:

Selections

Selection from *Earthwise at school*, by Linda Lowery and Marybeth Lorbiecki. Copyright © 1993 by Linda Lowery and Marybeth Lorbiecki. Reprinted by permission of Carolrhoda Books.

Family Pictures, written and illustrated by Carmen Lomas Garza. Copyright © 1990 by Carmen Lomas Garza. Reprinted by permission of Children's Books Press.

A Fruit & Vegetable Man, by Roni Schotter, illustrated by Jeanette Winter. Text copyright © 1993 by Roni Schotter. Illustrations copyright © 1993 by Jeanette Winter. Reprinted by permission of Little, Brown and Company.

"History Makers," from June/July 1993 *Kids Discover* magazine. Copyright © 1993 by Kids Discover. Reprinted by permission.

"Make Your Own Erupting Volcano," from *Science Wizardry for Kids*, by Margaret Kenda and Phyllis S. Williams. Copyright © 1992 by Margaret Kenda and Phyllis S. Williams. Reprinted by permission of Barrons Educational Series, Inc., Hauppage, NY.

Miss Nelson Is Missing!, by Harry Allard, illustrated by James Marshall. Text copyright © 1977 by Harry Allard. Illustrations copyright © 1977 by James Marshall. Reprinted by permission of Houghton Mifflin Company. All rights reserved.

"Molasses Tank Explosion Injures 50 and Kills 11," from the *Boston Daily Globe*, January 16, 1919. Public domain.

"My Hairy Neighbors," by Susan Lowell, from March 1994 *Ranger Rick* magazine. Copyright © 1994 by the National Wildlife Federation. Reprinted by permission.

Patrick and the Great Molasses Explosion, by Marjorie Stover. Copyright © 1985 by Dillon Press. Reprinted by permission of Silver Burdett Press.

Pompeii . . . Buried Alive! by Edith Kunhardt. Copyright © 1987 by Edith Kunhardt. Reprinted by permission of Random House, Inc.

"Pronunciation Key," from the *American Heritage Children's Dictionary*. Copyright © 1994 by Houghton Mifflin Company. Reprinted by permission. All rights reserved.

"This Little Piggy!" by Linda Granfield, from November 1992 *Owl* magazine. Copyright © 1992 by Linda Granfield. Reprinted by permission of the author and the Young Naturalist Foundation.

The Three Little Hawaiian Pigs and the Magic Shark, by Donivee Martin Laird. Copyright © 1981 by Donivee Martin Laird. Reprinted by permission of Barnaby Books, a Hawaii Partnership.

The Three Little Javelinas, by Susan Lowell. Illustrated by Jim Harris. Text copyright © 1992 by Susan Lowell. Illustrations copyright © 1992 by Jim Harris. Reprinted by permission of Northland Publishing, Flagstaff, AZ.

The Three Little Wolves and the Big Bad Pig, by Eugene Trivizas, illustrated by Helen Oxenbury. Text copyright © 1993 by Eugene Trivizas. Illustrations copyright © 1993 by Helen Oxenbury. Reprinted by permission of Margaret K. McElderry Books, Simon & Schuster Children's Publishing Division. First published by Heinemann Young Books in Great Britain.

The Titanic, adapted and arranged by Alan Lomax. Copyright © renewed 1964 by Ludlow Music, Inc., New York, NY. Reprinted by permission.

The Titanic: Lost . . . and Found, by Judy Donnelly. Copyright © 1987 by Judy Donnelly. Reprinted by permission of Random House, Inc.

Titanic Trivia, by A.F.J. Marshello. Copyright © 1987 by A.F.J. Marshello. Reprinted by permission of the Titanic Historical Society, Inc., Indian Orchard, MA 01151.

"What's Up, Pup?" by Lyle Prescott, from July 1994 *Ranger Rick* magazine. Copyright © 1994 by the National Wildlife Federation. Reprinted by permission.

"The Wild Boar & the Fox," from *Aesop's Fables: Plays for Young Children,* by Dr. Albert Cullum. Copyright © 1993 by Fearon Teacher Aids, a Paramount Communications Company. Reprinted by permission of Paramount Communications.

When Jo Louis Won the Title, by Belinda Rochelle, illustrated by Larry Johnson. Text copyright © 1994 by Belinda Rochelle. Illustrations copyright © 1994 by Larry Johnson. Reprinted by permission of Houghton Mifflin Company. All rights reserved.

Poetry

"Away from Town," from *Runny Days, Sunny Days*, by Aileen Fisher. Copyright © 1958 by Aileen Fisher. Reprinted by permission of the author.

"City," by Langston Hughes, from *The Langston Hughes Reader.* Copyright © 1958 by Langston Hughes. Copyright renewed 1986 by George Houston Bass. Reprinted by permission of Harold Ober Associates, Inc.

"Pigs," by Charles Ghigna, from January 1993 *Ranger Rick* magazine. Copyright © 1993 by Charles Ghigna. Reprinted by permission of the author.

Additional Acknowledgments

Special thanks to the following teachers whose students' compositions are included in the Be a Writer features in this level:

David Burton, Blake Lower School, Hopkins, Minnesota; Linda Chick, Paloma Elementary School, San Marcos, California; Debora Adam, South Dover Elementary School, Dover, Delaware

CREDITS

Illustration **12–27** James Marshall; **37–59** Helen Oxenbury; **88** Renee Lynn/Photo Researchers **92–113** Don Stuart; **115** Brian Lies; **118–119** Loretta Lustig; **127–144** Jeanette Winter; **151–179** Carmen Lomas Garza; **181** Pam Rossi; **184** Pam Rossi; **189–210** Larry Johnson; **225–247** John Gamache; **254–274** Robert G. Steele; **285–304** Brad Teare

Photography **28** Courtesy of Harry Allard (tl); Houghton Mifflin Co. (tr) **36** Courtesy of Helen Oxenbury; Courtesy of Eugene Trivizas and Reed Childrens Books (t); ©Otto Rogge/The Stock Market (t,b) **61** Ranger Rick Magazine; Art Wolfe **62** Art Wolfe (tr,bl) **63** Art Wolfe (tr,b); Ranger Rick Magazine (b) **64** © Andrew Sacks/©Tony Stone Images/Chicago Inc **65** ©David Falconer/DRK Photo (t); John Colwell/Grant Heilman Photography (b) **66** The Bettmann Archive (t); ©Andrew Sacks/Tony Stone Images/Chicago Inc (b) **67** ©Stephen J. Krasemann/DRK Photo (t); ©Phil Dotson/Photo Researchers (t); Alain Compost/Bruce Coleman Inc (t); Robert Barclay/Grant Heilman Photography (b) **68-69** Mark Muench/©Tony Stone Images/Chicago Inc **68** Ross Humphreys/ Courtesy of Susan Lowell (t); Courtesy of Jim Harris (b) **88** Renee Lynn/Photo Researchers **89** Thomas A. Wiewandt (tr) **90-91** Thomas A. Wiewandt **92** Courtesy of Donivee M. Laird (tl); Courtesy of Don Stuart (br) **117** Courtesy of Kara Johnson **126** Courtesy of Roni Schotter (tl); Courtesy of Jeanette Winter (br) **146-9** Fred Boyles **182-183** ©Ken Biggs/©Tony Stone Images/Chicago Inc **213** Courtesy of Joyce Hsieh **214** Little, Brown & Co. **215** Francine Seders Gallery LTD **216** Nat. Museum of the American Indian **217** The Cleveland Museum of Art **218-19** Joanna McArthy/The Image Bank **220-21** G. Brad Lewis/©Tony Stone Images/Chicago Inc **222-23** © G. Brad Lewis/©Tony Stone Images/Chicago Inc **224** Courtesy of Judy Donnelly; Courtesy of John Gamache **227** Courtesy of The Mariners Museum, Newport News, Virginia (br); Ken Marschall Collection/The Illustrated London News (bl) **228** Courtesy of The Mariners Museum, Newport News, Virginia; Brown Brothers (tl, tr); Ken Marschall Collection/Harland & Wolfe (br) **231** Brown Brothers (br) **232** Stock Montage, Inc. (br); Brown Brothers (bl) **235** Brown Brothers (br) **237** Bruce Dale©/National Geographic Society (b); The Bettmann Archive (ml) **239** The Illustrated London News Picture Library (m) **240** Brown Brothers (bl) **241** Brown Brothers (m); The Bettmann Archive (m); Hulton Deutsch (br) **242** Stock Montage, Inc. (m); Brown Brothers (m) **243** The Bettmann Archive (ml); Brown Brothers (mr) **245** R. Sobol/Sipa Press (bl) **246** Emory Kristof/National Geographic Society (tl) **246-7** ©Woods Hole Oceanographic Inst. **248** Courtesy of The Mariners Museum, Newport News, Virginia (m) **250** Courtesy of The Mariners Museum, Newport News, Virginia (tr); Brown Brothers (mr); The Bettmann Archive (bl, bm) **251** Ken Marschall Collection (tr) **254** Courtesy of Edith Kundhardt (t) **254** Courtesy of Robert Steele (b) **271** ©O.L. Mazzatenta/National Geographic Society (tl); ©David Hiser/Photographers/Aspen (b) **272** ©Jonathan Blair/National Geographic Society **273** C M Dixon (ml); (c); David Hiser/Photographers/Aspen (b) **274** ©Roy Rainford/Robert Harding Picture Library **276** ©E.R. Degginger/Allstock (bl); Tony Waltham/Robert Harding Picture Library (br) **277** Reuters/Bettmann/The Bettmann Archive (t); The Bettmann Archive (ml) **278** ©Sipa Press (tr); Ralph Perry/Allstock (br); The Bettmann Archive (bl) **279** ©Robert Fried/Robert Fried Photography (tr); UPI/Bettmann/The Bettmann Archive (bl); ©Gary Braasch (br) **282** Courtesy of Marcus Grant **284** John Stover/ Courtesy of Marjorie Stover (tl); Courtesy of Brad Teare (br) **306** Boston Globe **307-9** Bostonian Society **312** The Image Bank (l) **313** Joe Szkoozinski/The Image Bank (l) **314** M. Dwyer/Stock Boston (r) **315** Charles Allen/The Image Bank (r) **317** Patti Murrray/Animals Animals (l); Peter Henorie/The Image Bank (r)

Assignment Photography **6–7** Tony Scarpetta **8–9, 10–11** Glenn Kremer **28** Tracey Wheeler **29–35** Tony Scarpetta **36** Dave Desroches **60** Tony Scarpetta **114** Banta Digital Group; Tracey Wheeler **116–117** Tony Scarpetta **120–121** Tracey Wheeler **122–123, 124–125, 126–127** Tony Scarpetta **145** Tracey Wheeler **150–151** Glenn Kremer **180, 184–185** Tony Scarpetta **185** Tracey Wheeler (insets) **186–187** Tony Scarpetta **188** Katherine Lambert **211** Tracey Wheeler **212–213** Tony Scarpetta **214–215, 216–217** Banta Digital Group **224** Tony Scarpetta (insets) **248, 249, 250–251, 275** Banta Digital Group **280** Tony Scarpetta **281** Tracey Wheeler **282–283** Banta Digital Group **284** Kindra Clineff **305** Banta Digital Group; Tracey Wheeler (inset) **306, 307, 308–309** Banta Digital Group

Here's what visitors to our Web site said about stories in *Enjoy.*

The Three Little Hawaiian Pigs and the Magic Shark is the best book I have ever read! It has Hawaiian words in it. I like the illustrations. If I met the Hawaiian pigs, I would speak Hawaiian to them.

Ryan Leaird, North Carolina

I like the book *Pompeii . . . Buried Alive!* It was very exciting when the volcano erupted. My favorite part of *Pompeii . . . Buried Alive!* is when the volcano erupted. My favorite character in this story is Vesuvius the volcano. I like this story because it makes you feel like you're right in the story.

Jacob Klehr, Minnesota

Post your reviews in the

Kids' Clubhouse

at

www.eduplace.com